Trees and Shrubs
of Colorado

Trees and Shrubs
of Colorado

Jack L. Carter

Illustrated by Marjorie C. Leggitt

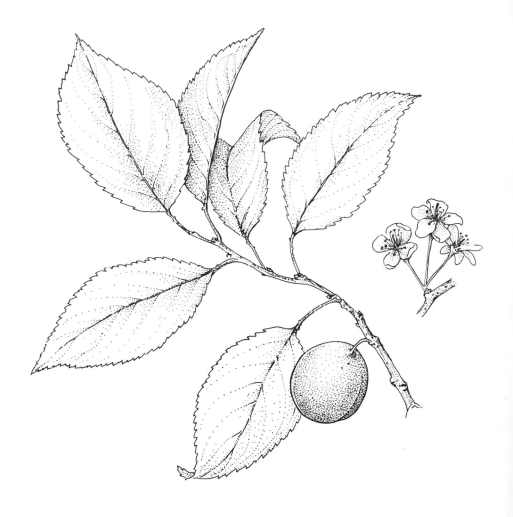

Johnson Books, Distributor: Boulder

ISBN 0-9619945-0-9

Library of Congress Catalog Card Number: 88-070830

Distributed by Johnson Books
1880 South 57th Court
Boulder, Colorado 80301
(303) 443-1576 and
Jack L. Carter
Department of Biology, The Colorado College
Colorado Springs, Colorado 80903

Cover illustration and book design
by Marjorie C. Leggitt
Leggitt Design Ltd.

Cover illustration:
WESTERN SALTBUSH
Atriplex corrugata
p. 66

Table of Contents

Introduction

About my fourth year as a faculty member at The Colorado College, George Drake, Dean of the College, expressed his concern about the increased enrollments in the beginning botany and field botany courses. His questions to me were: "When will this increased enrollment in botany courses level off?" "When will you be satisfied with enrollments?" My response: "When every person who graduates from our nation's schools and colleges has completed a basic botany course."

Plants are the life-sustaining connection between *Homo sapiens* and planet earth. Yet the average, upper middle class citizen spends far more time and money killing plants and cutting grass and wood than becoming familiar with the native plants in his or her environment. Humankind struggles, in the Biblical sense, for "dominion over life on earth" rather than learning to live with the earth.

While most economic cycles are based on products that generally result in dumps and landfills; biologic cycles do not produce waste products. From the time a seed germinates until the tree dies, there are no lost natural resources. In fact, in life and in death, plants contribute to other forms of life on planet earth. Although not always balanced, life cycles result in a steady-state system. Humankind has never been able to develop steady-state economic cycles that can live with nature; rather, our economic cycles continue to destroy the natural world.

We, along with all plants and other animals, have evolved together over millions of years. We are on this planet together and the survival of all life is closely interrelated. Yet we fail as a species to teach the young the connections between the survival of *Homo sapiens* and the survival of natural environments.

There are those, however, who want to know more, and have questions concerning the local flora. A week seldom passes during the growing season that I fail to receive several inquiries from local people about the flora of Colorado. These questions come from thoughtful and intelligent people who have a limited knowledge of the local flora. They may be fishing, hiking, camping, or just walking the city streets, and come across plants that are new or of special interest to them. In recent years I have received more and more requests for information about native trees and shrubs that can survive in lawns and gardens on normal annual moisture without additional water. These inquiries are important because they tell me people are becoming concerned about water consumption. For every question answered, however, there must be many people with other related questions on the flora of Colorado that go unanswered.

Successful teachers free their students from their guidance so that the students can work independent of the teacher. The major objective of this book is to help interested students help themselves. This book is designed to assist those who want to become familiar with some of the native and introduced trees, shrubs, and woody vines of the Colorado Rocky Mountains and the adjacent plains, but do not have a teacher available.

TREES AND SHRUBS OF COLORADO includes woody plants in a well-defined, central area of Colorado. The term "woody," although somewhat ambiguous, is defined here as plants with woody stems which extend several centimeters or more above the soil line; woody vines are included. I have attempted to include the native and naturalized woody species, as well as a number of the commonly cultivated species. Obviously, it is impossible to include every single woody species, and new cultivars are being brought into the state continuously. Extensive field work with field botany classes at The Colorado College, however, has revealed few woody species that are not included.

The most effective range for this book is approximately a 150-mile radius of Pikes Peak. This area includes the Front Range from Fort Collins to the southern border of the state, east to Limon and Lamar on the plains, and west to Eagle, Gunnison, and Del Norte. As you move to the four corners of the state and to the western slope, the book becomes less effective. I have included several woody members of the Asteraceae (sunflower family) and the Chenopodiaceae (goosefoot family) that occur in southern Colorado. Those species are difficult for beginning students to identify with other available literature.

Identifying plants is very different from identifying birds and large mammals: sight identifications are more difficult and the vocabulary required to use even a simple dichotomous key to woody plants extends beyond the normal vocabulary of most beginning students. For this reason I have included a glossary, as well as a pictorial glossary.

What is a dichotomous key? Keys are useful devices in identifying an unknown. The conventional type of key to unknown plants and animals is the dichotomous key. The term dichotomous denotes two divisions or two choices. This means the specimen under consideration, if it is a woody plant collected or observed in Colorado, should be described in one of the two number ones at the beginning of the key. If the plant is described in the first number one you should proceed to number two; but, if the plant is described in the second number one you should by-pass number two and move to the designated number. At the end of each couplet, you are directed to the next couplet appropriate to the specimen you are keying. Always read both statements in the couplet.

If you are familiar with the major life zones in Colorado, and the elevations that limit those life zones, it will be much easier to use TREES AND SHRUBS OF COLORADO. In each plant description we have identified the life zone(s) and the elevation range in which the plant occurs. As you identify the woody plants included in this key, note the approximate elevation and life zone in which the species occurs.

The life zones are limited as follows:

Plains: The altitude ranges from approximately 4,000 feet on the eastern border of the state to 6,000 feet in the front range. With the exception of the cottonwood-willow riparian ecosystem and the sagebrush, yucca, rabbitbrush, and four-winged saltbrush of the drier areas, trees and shrubs are not abundant on the plains.

Foothills: The altitude ranges from 5,700 feet to 8,200 feet in central Colorado. Mountain mahogany, Gambel's oak, red cedar, wax currant, and kinnikinnik characterize this zone. Because of the abundance of woody shrubs some authors have identified this life zone as the shrub zone.

Montane: The altitude ranges from approximately 8,000 feet to 9,500 feet over most of Colorado, but this varies from the southern to the northern borders of Colorado. Sometimes referred to as the Ponderosa Pine--Douglas-fir Zone, it is important to distinguish the direction of the slope. In the montane, a dry, south-facing slope will usually be characterized by the Ponderosa Pine, while on the cooler, north-facing slopes you find the Douglas-fir in greater abundance. Also, in the northern part of the state and on the western slope the Douglas-fir becomes the predominant tree of the montane.

Subalpine: The altitude ranges from approximately 9,200 feet to 11,000 feet over most of Colorado. Rich in available moisture and identified by the lush growth of trees and shrubs, this is the region visitors to Colorado most enjoy. Engelmann Spruce and the Subalpine Fir are characteristic of the subalpine zone. The Bristlecone Pine (Foxtail Pine) and the Limber Pine are distributed widely throughout these elevations. At the upper elevations of the subalpine the timberline is characterized by tree "flagging" or "Krummholz." Several authors have identified this life zone as the flower garden of the Rocky Mountains.

Alpine Tundra: Starting from around 10,500 to 11,000 feet to above 14,000 feet this zone forms the top of the Rockies. Extremely cold, dry, windswept conditions are reflected in dwarfed and matted plants growing from deep root systems. It is interesting to note that the grasses and sedges are an important part of this flora, as they are on the plains. Students of the alpine tundra sometimes refer to this fascinating life zone as a high altitude desert. There are no trees in the tundra, and the few shrubs reside low and close to the ground.

Once you have conquered the terms necessary to start to move through the keys, the extensive illustrations become extremely helpful. Initiated during a flowering plant course at The Colorado College, Marjorie Leggitt assumed responsibility for illustrating the plants that would be included in the keys. Over a period of eleven years as the manual developed, she used live specimens and herbarium sheets to produce over 150 illustrations. The Colorado College students who tested earlier drafts of the manual praised Ms. Leggitt's work.

Two other former students played important roles in the preparation of this manual. Harry M. Stover produced the illustrations for the key to the gymnosperms, and Katherine Ake assisted in the development and editing of the manuscript. Beyond these two people, who had major responsibilities, a complete list of the students, faculty, and friends who have in one way or another contributed to the development of this small book would be a roster of names longer than the total list of included species. I am extremely grateful for their assistance. At the same time there are errors and omissions in this guide; for those I accept full responsibility.

There is a hidden agenda within the covers of this small book. I believe those who know and appreciate the inner relationships among living things, exemplified by the flora and fauna of Colorado, will develop an appreciation for this beautiful state and the total environment. An informed society just might come to treasure an undisturbed short-grass prairie or a pinyon-juniper forest over another shopping center or a new airport. Clean air and water may become, with time, more important to Colorado than the next government contract or a new industry. I believe that informed people will understand limits to growth and vote for alternatives to the growthmania sweeping Colorado.

Jack L. Carter
1 January 1988

Preliminary Key

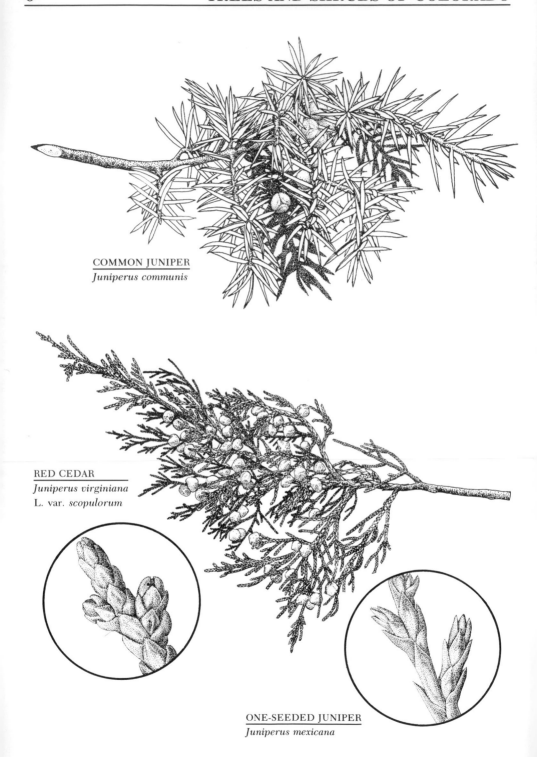

COMMON JUNIPER
Juniperus communis

RED CEDAR
Juniperus virginiana
L. var. *scopulorum*

ONE-SEEDED JUNIPER
Juniperus mexicana

KEY I

Gymnosperms

1. Leaves small, awl-like, scale-like or imbricate, not needle-like; fruit a berry at maturity 2

1. Leaves needle-like, separate or in clusters, not scale-like or imbricate; fruit a dry or woody cone at maturity 4

    2. Leaves on mature branches awl-shaped, not imbricate, 5 to 15 mm long; shrubs usually less than 1 meter high, spreading and prostrate; common over the western third of Colorado, from 5,000 to 7,500 ft (1524 to 2286 m).

    COMMON JUNIPER, *Juniperus communis* L.   (Cupressaceae)

    2. Leaves on mature branches imbricate and scale-like, not awl-shaped, less than 6 mm long; trees or shrubs usually more than 1 meter high, growing upright from a single trunk 3

3. Leaves entire, occurring in pairs under hand lens, light or gray-green; fruit green or purple containing 1 to 3, usually 2 seeds; heartwood purple or red; branchlets extended, long and slender in growth habit.

    RED CEDAR, *Juniperus virginiana* L. var. *scopulorum* Lemmon (**EAST-ERN RED CEDAR,** *Juniperus virginiana* L., is introduced and cultivated in lawns throughout the area)   (Cupressaceae)

3. Leaves minutely denticulate, occurring in pairs or whorls under hand lens, dark green; fruit green or purple, containing 1 to 2, often 1 seed; heartwood brown; branchlets shorter and stout in growth habit.

    ONE-SEEDED JUNIPER, *Juniperus mexicana* Spreng. var. *mono-sperma* (Englem.) Cory   (Cupressaceae)

    4. Needles in clusters or fascicles containing 2 or more needles; base surrounded by a sheath 5

    4. Needles separate, not in clusters or fascicles; base not surrounded by a sheath 9

5. Needles in clusters or fascicles of 5 6

5. Needles in clusters or fascicles of 2 or 3 7

6.   Needles usually more than 4 cm long, straight or slightly curved, not sticky to the touch; cone scales lacking prickles; seed wings rudimentary or absent; foothills to subalpine, 5,000 to 11,000 ft (1524 to 3353 m).

     LIMBER PINE, *Pinus flexilis* James   (Pinaceae)

6.   Needles usually less than 4 cm long, curved, with gray-green resin spots, sticky to touch; cone scales with exserted prickles; seeds winged; montane to subalpine, 7,000 to 13,000 ft (2134 to 3962 m).

     BRISTLECONE or FOXTAIL PINE, *Pinus aristata* Engelm.   (Pinaceae)

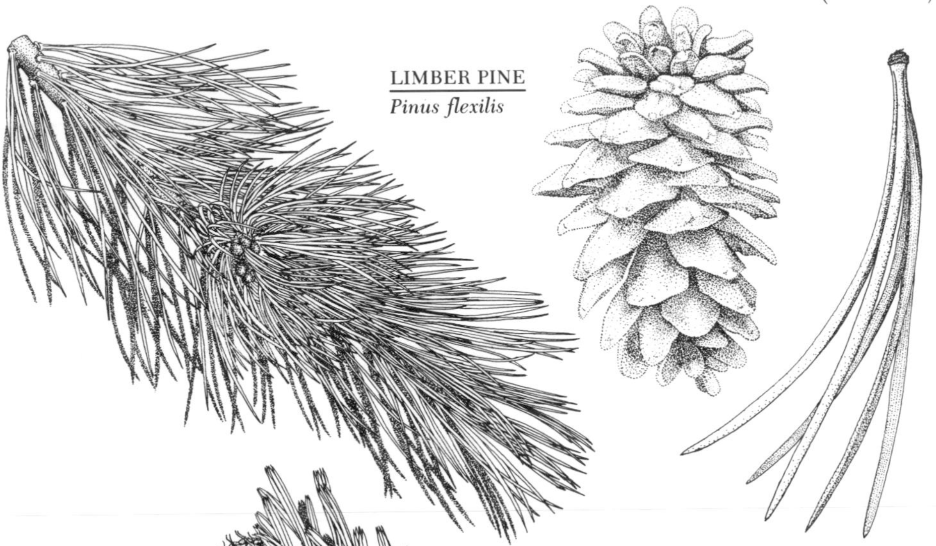

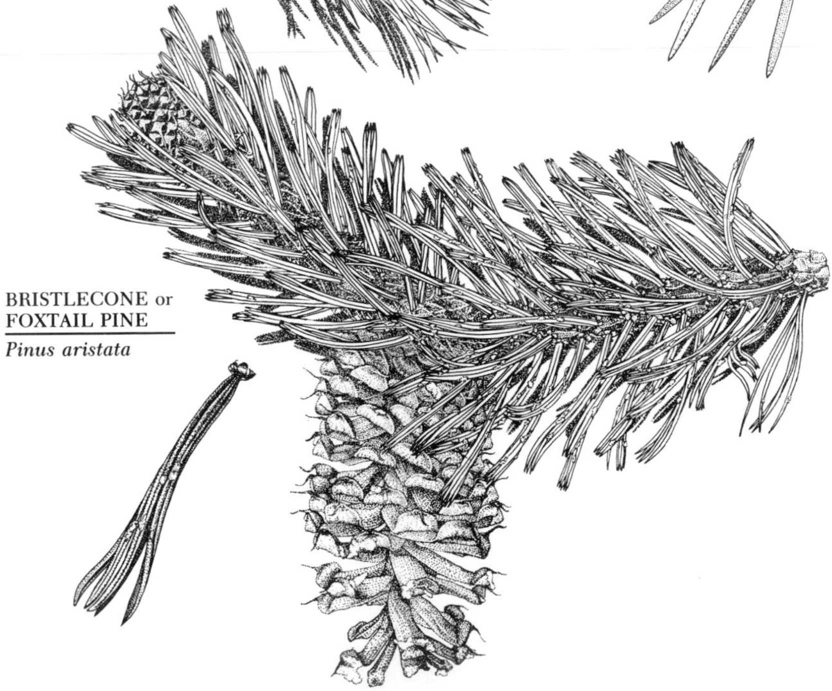

LIMBER PINE
Pinus flexilis

BRISTLECONE or
FOXTAIL PINE
Pinus aristata

7.   Needles 8 to 20 cm long; cones 7 to 13 cm long; mesas to montane, 5,000
     to 9,000 ft (1524 to 2743 m).

     PONDEROSA PINE, *Pinus ponderosa* Dougl. ex Laws.   (Pinaceae)

7.   Needles less than 8 cm long; cones less than 6 cm long 8

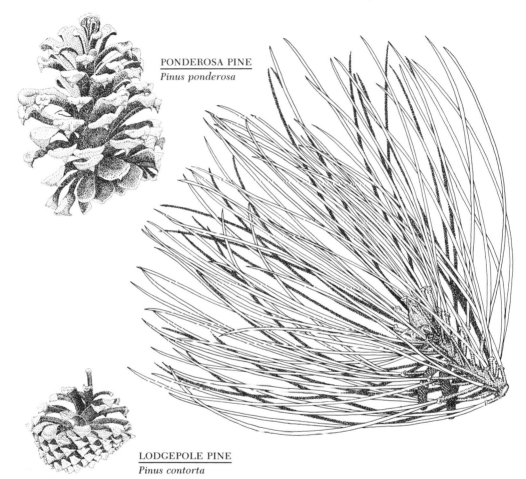

PONDEROSA PINE
Pinus ponderosa

LODGEPOLE PINE
Pinus contorta

8.   Cone scales bristle-tipped; cones persistent; tree tall, slender, usu-
     ally over 18 m tall at maturity; commonly occurring in, but not
     restricted to, burned-over areas, above 8,000 ft (2438 m) in our area.

     LODGEPOLE PINE, *Pinus contorta* Dougl.   (Pinaceae)

8.   Cone scales not bristle-tipped; cones falling at maturity; trees less
     than 16 m tall; not confined to burned-over areas; occurring at 4,000
     to 9,000 ft (1219 to 2743 m) in our area.

     PINYON PINE, *Pinus edulis* Engelm.   (Pinaceae)

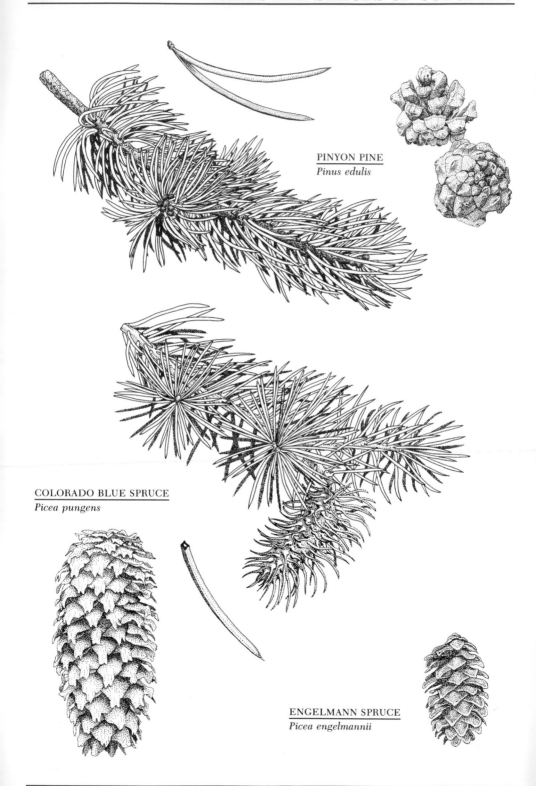

PINYON PINE
Pinus edulis

COLORADO BLUE SPRUCE
Picea pungens

ENGELMANN SPRUCE
Picea engelmannii

9. Needles mostly 4 sided; branchlets roughened by persistent leaf bases; leaves deciduous when specimens are dry 10

9. Needles flattened or 2-sided; branchlets not roughened by persistent leaf bases; leaves not deciduous when specimens are dry. 11

10. Needles rigid, sharp to the touch, almost spine-tipped; cones over 6 cm long; needles often with obvious bluish color, giving tree a bluish caste; occurring in foothills to montane at 7,000 to 9,500 ft (2134 to 2896 m). This is the state tree of Colorado.

COLORADO BLUE SPRUCE, *Picea pungens* Engelm.   (Pinaceae)

10. Needles somewhat flexible, not very sharp to the touch or spine-tipped; cones less than 6 cm long; bluish color not as obvious; trees of upper montane and subalpine at elevations of 8,500 to 12,000 ft (2591 to 3658 m).

ENGLEMANN SPRUCE, *Picea engelmannii* Parry ex Engelm.

(Pinaceae)

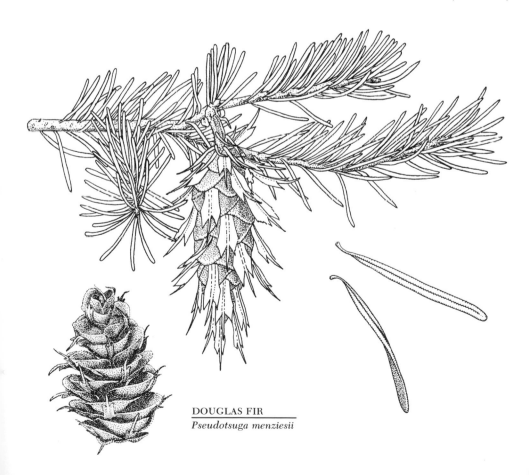

DOUGLAS FIR
Pseudotsuga menziesii

11. Needles slightly petioled or stalked; leaf scars elliptic to oval, occasionally extending down the stem below the point of attachment; cones pendulous, the scales persistent with long exserted bracts.

DOUGLAS FIR, *Pseudotsuga menziesii* (Mirbel) Franco   (Pinaceae)

11. Needles sessile; leaf scars orbicular, not extending down the stem below the point of attachment; cones erect, the scales deciduous without long exserted bracts 12

12. Needles averaging 3 cm or more in length; resin ducts in needles near the epidermis; cones grayish-green, 7 to 12 cm long; bracts of the cone-scales with short triangular tips; occurring at lower elevations, 7,500 to 10,000 ft (2286 to 3048 m).

WHITE FIR, *Abies concolor* (Gord. & Glend.) Lindl.   (Pinaceae)

12. Needles averaging 2 cm or less in length; resin ducts in needles near the center and inside the epidermis; cones dark purple, 5 to 10 cm long; bracts of the cone-scales with long awl-shaped tips; occurring at higher elevations, 8,500 to 12,000 ft (2591 to 3658 m).

SUBALPINE FIR, *Abies lasiocarpa* (Hook.) Nutt.   (Pinaceae)

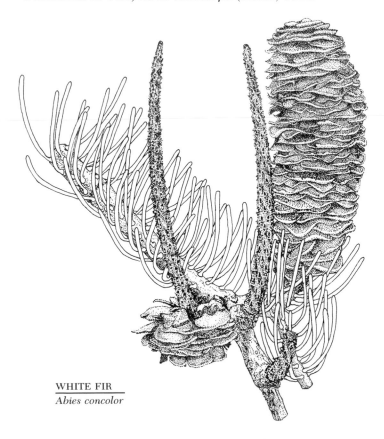

WHITE FIR
Abies concolor

KEY II

Simple, Opposite or Whorled, Broad Leaves

1. Leaves lobed 2
1. Leaves not lobed 7

    2. Leaves palmately lobed, occasionally some leaves 3 parted 3

    2. Leaves pinnately lobed (genus *Symphoricarpos* Duhamel) 27

3. Mature leaves less than 7.0 cm in width, margins toothed to finely serrated or dentated 4
3. Mature leaves more than 7.0 cm in width, margins rarely somewhat toothed but never finely serrated 5

    4. Young twigs gray to brown in color; fruit a 1-seeded drupe becoming red at maturity; leaves usually 3 lobed but often without lobes; shrubs 1.0 to 2.0 m tall; infrequent, from 7,000 to 9,000 ft (2134 to 2743 m). A similar species, *Viburnum pauciflorum* La Pylaie ex T. & G., is commonly cultivated throughout the area and will also key out here.

    HIGH BUSH CRANBERRY, *Viburnum edule* (Michx.) Raf.

    (Caprifoliaceae)

HIGH BUSH CRANBERRY
Viburnum edule

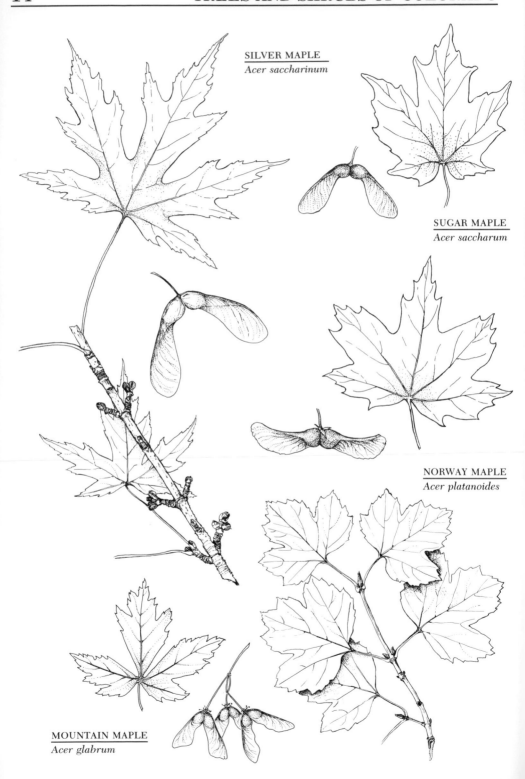

SILVER MAPLE
Acer saccharinum

SUGAR MAPLE
Acer saccharum

NORWAY MAPLE
Acer platanoides

MOUNTAIN MAPLE
Acer glabrum

4. Young twigs red in color; fruit of 2 united samaras, wings 2.0 to 3.0 cm long; leaves 3 to 5 lobed or occasionally palmately divided into 3 separate leaflets, both leaf arrangements can be found on the same plant; shrubs or small trees up to 8.0 m tall; native species frequent along streams, from 5,000 to 10,500 ft (1524 to 3200 m).

MOUNTAIN MAPLE, *Acer glabrum* Torr.   (Aceraceae)

5. Spaces (sinuses) between the main lobes of the leaves deeply V-shaped forming a definite angle; leaves 5 lobed, silvery white beneath; samaras falling before the leaves are full grown; introduced to Colorado.

SILVER MAPLE, *Acer saccharinum* L.   (Aceraceae)

5. Spaces (sinuses) between the main lobes of the leaves shallowly U-shaped, rounded, not forming a definite angle 6

6. Samara wings diverging at an angle of about 180°; juice milky (best seen at the base of a detached petiole); buds green or red, stout or blunt; introduced to Colorado.

NORWAY MAPLE, *Acer platanoides* L.   (Aceraceae)

6. Samara wings diverging at angles of less than 120° or at right angles to the pedicel; juice not milky; buds brown, slender and acute; introduced to Colorado.

SUGAR MAPLE, *Acer saccharum* Marsh   (Aceraceae)

7. Stems creeping or prostrate, if erect then plant less than 15.0 cm tall; shrubs or herbaceous plants seldom to 40.0 cm tall 8

7. Stems erect; shrubs or trees usually over 40.0 cm tall 13

8. Leaf margins entire, occasionally somewhat revolute 9

8. Leaf margins crenate or serrate, at least above the middle 11

9. Stems erect, herbaceous, occurring singly from woody rhizomes; leaves in a whorl near top of stem; inflorescence subtended by 4 to 5, white, petal-like bracts; plants herbaceous, less than 15.0 cm tall; uncommon, occurring in deep shade of subalpine forests, 7,500 to 11,000 ft (2286 to 3353 m).

BUNCHBERRY, DWARF CORNEL, *Chamaepericlymenum canadense* (L.) Aschers. et Graebn. (previously: *Cornus canadensis* L.)   (Cornaceae)

9. Stems creeping or prostrate, forming low diffusely branched shrubs or mats from woody rhizomes; leaves opposite; inflorescence lacking subtending petal-like bracts 10

10. Leaves less than 1.5 cm long at maturity, revolute, nearly or quite sessile; plant native to Colorado from 9,000 to 11,500 ft (2743 to 3505 m).

LAUREL, *Kalmia polifolia* Wang.   (Ericaceae)

10. Leaves more than 2.0 cm long at maturity, not revolute, with short petioles, seldom sessile; plant introduced to Colorado, commonly cultivated in lawns and gardens.

PERIWINKLE, *Vinca minor* L.   (Apocynaceae)

11. Leaves more than 3.0 cm long, broadly oblanceolate to nearly obovate, sometimes appearing whorled; frequent in shaded cool areas, 8,000 to 11,500 ft (2438 to 3505 m).

PIPSISSEWA, *Chimaphila umbellata* (L.) Bart.   (Pyrolaceae)

11. Leaves less than 3.0 cm long, oval or elliptic to oblong, opposite, never whorled; plants of wooded hillsides, 6,000 to 11,000 ft (1829 to 3353 m) ... 12

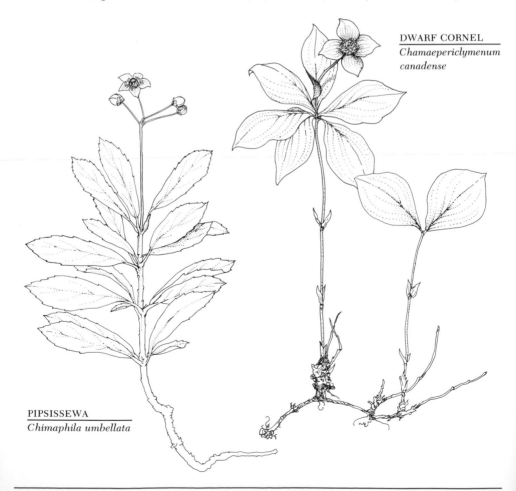

DWARF CORNEL
Chamaepericlymenum canadense

PIPSISSEWA
Chimaphila umbellata

12.   Leaves crenate above the middle; younger stems pubescent forming loose mats; flowers in pairs in erect stalks; shrubs seldom more than 20.0 cm tall; native plant of moist woods from 8,500 to 11,000 ft (2591 to 3353 m).

TWINFLOWER, *Linnaea borealis* L.   (Caprifoliaceae)

12.   Leaves serrate above the middle; younger stems glabrous; flowers inconspicuous, sessile in leaf axils; shrubs up to 40.0 cm tall; native plant of wooded slopes, from 8,500 to 11,000 ft (2591 to 3353 m).

MOUNTAIN LOVER, *Pachistima myrsinites* (Pursh) Raf.   (Celastraceae)

13.   Margin of leaves entire 14

13.   Margn of leaves never entire, usually serrate, dentate or undulate 32

14.   Mature leaves less than 1.0 cm wide and 4.0 cm long 15

14.   Mature leaves more than 1.0 cm wide and 3.0 cm long 22

15.   Plant of subalpine and alpine, from 9,000 to 11,500 ft (2743 to 3505 m); leaves evergreen, 1.0 to 2.0 cm long, oval to elliptic-oblong; shrubs low, diffusely branching, to 20.0 cm high.

LAUREL, *Kalmia polifolia* Wang.   (Ericaceae)

15.   Plants of plains, foothills, and lower montane, to 9,000 ft (2743 m) 16

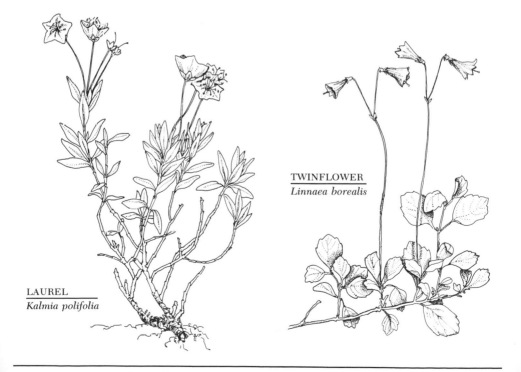

TWINFLOWER
Linnaea borealis

LAUREL
Kalmia polifolia

16.   Shrubs woody at the base becoming herbaceous above or new growth herbaceous in first season; mature stems 7.0 to 35.0 cm tall; leaves opposite, sometimes becoming alternate above, linear to lanceolate, 0.5 to 3.0 cm long 17

16.   Shrubs woody throughout; mature stems 30.0 to 200.0 cm tall, leaves opposite throughout, linear oblong to ovate, 0.5 to 4.0 cm long 18

17. Mature leaves 1.5 to 3.0 cm long, linear to lanceolate, opposite, sometimes becoming alternate above; flowers perfect, in cymes, yellow, stamens 2; fruit a two valved capsule; dry areas in southern part of state; 5,000 to 6,000 ft (1525 to 1830 m).

MENDORA, *Menodora scabra* (Engelm.) A. Gray   (Oleaceae)

17. Mature leaves 0.5 to 1.2 cm long, linear and in fascicles in the axils of older, primary leaves, not becoming alternate; flowers perfect, regular, solitary, white, stamens 6; fruit a capsule surrounded by the calyx; dry hills and plains in the southern third of state; 4,000 to 5,500 ft (1219 to 1675 m).

MOCKHEATHER, *Frankenia jamesii* Torr.   (Frankeniaceae)

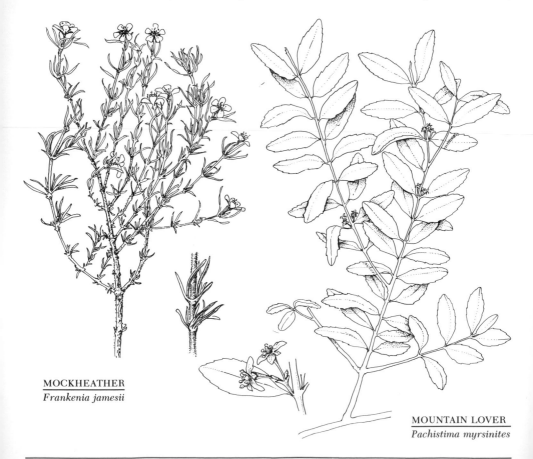

MOCKHEATHER
Frankenia jamesii

MOUNTAIN LOVER
Pachistima myrsinites

MENODORA
Monodora scabra

18.   Shrubs with spiny, rough, much branched and rigid stems; mature leaves fleshy, linear or linear filiform, 1.0 to 4.0 cm long; fruit with winged margins; plant of alkaline flats, south of Colorado Springs.

GREASEWOOD, *Sarcobatus vermiculatus* (Hook.) Torr.

(Chenopodiaceae)

18.   Shrubs without spines, but occasionally rough due to the shredding or exfoliating of the bark; mature leaves oblong, lanceolate, ovate, or orbicular, 0.5 to 3.0 cm long; fruit without winged margins 19

19.   Fruit a capsule; stamens 8 to 15 or more; leaves oblong to lanceolate or slightly ovate, often characterized by 3 main veins from near the base 20

19.   Fruit a 2-seeded berry-like drupe; stamens 4 or 5; leaves elliptical to orbicular or slightly ovate, 1 main vein from near the base 21

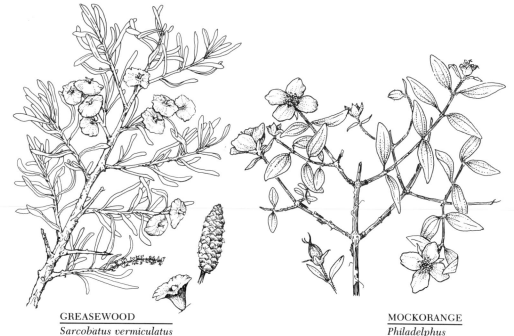

GREASEWOOD
Sarcobatus vermiculatus

MOCKORANGE
Philadelphus

20.   Fruit an obovoid or obconic capsule, the beaks rising abruptly from the body; stamens 15 or more; young twigs brown to gray. One native species in our area, *Philadelphus microphyllus* A. Gray, but also several introduced species are cultivated in lawns and gardens.

MOCKORANGE, *Philadelphus* L.   (Saxifragaceae)

20.   Fruit a conic or ovoid capsule, the beaks tapering gradually from the body; stamens 8; young branches with tan to reddish-brown bark; plant on rocky slopes, southern Colorado; 4,000 to 8,000 ft (1219 to 2440 m).

FENDLERBUSH, *Fendlera rupicola* A. Gray   (Saxifragaceae)

FENDLERBUSH
Fendlera rupicola

21.   Corolla tubular or funnel-shaped, the lobes much shorter than the tube; young twigs glabrous; shrubs 100.0 to 150.0 cm tall.

SNOWBERRY, BUCKBRUSH, *Symphoricarpos oreophilus* A. Gray

(Caprifoliaceae)

21.   Corolla campanulate, the lobes about as long as or slightly longer than the tube; young twigs pubescent with short curved hairs; shrubs 20.0 to 80.0 cm tall.

SNOWBERRY, BUCKBRUSH, *Symphoricarpos albus* (L.) Blake

(Caprifoliaceae)

22.   Mature leaves whorled, more than 15.0 cm long and 12.0 cm wide; fruit a capsule, 2.0 to 5.0 dm long, 1.0 to 1.5 cm thick; trees up to 30.0 m tall; introduced and cultivated in urban areas throughout Colorado.

CATALPA, *Catalpa speciosa* Warder   (Bignoniaceae)

22.   Mature leaves opposite, seldom whorled, less than 15.0 cm long and 12.0 cm wide; fruit variable; trees or shrubs 23

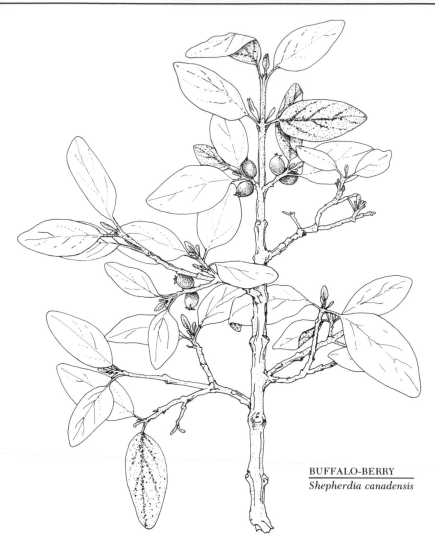

BUFFALO-BERRY
Shepherdia canadensis

23.   Leaves and twigs covered with silvery or rusty scales, green above, scurfy with brown glandular spots below; fruit yellowish-red, inedible; native plant from 7,500 to 11,000 ft (2286 to 3353 m).

BUFFALO-BERRY, *Shepherdia canadensis* (L.) Nutt.   (Elaeagnaceae)

Another species in the Eleagnaceae, *Shepherdia argentea* (Pursh) Nutt., occurs over the western two-thirds of the state. This species is silvery-scurfy over both surfaces of the leaf and lacks the brown glandular spots that aid in the identification of *Shepherdia canadensis* (L.) Nutt. Also, the leaves are 2.5 to 5.0 cm. long and oblong to obtuse in shape. *Shepherdia argentea* may become a small tree reaching 3.0 m and thorns may be present.

23.   Leaves and twigs not covered with a silvery or rusty scales, not scurfy below 24

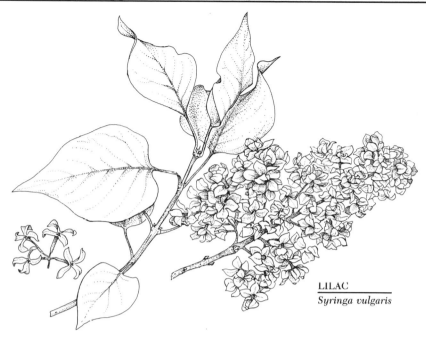

LILAC
Syringa vulgaris

24.   Leaves 5.0 to 10.0 cm long, ovate, base cordate or subcordate, tapering to a tip; introduced shrub of lawns and old home sites, spreading by roots.

   LILAC, *Syringa vulgaris* L.   (Oleaceae)

24.   Leaves not with the above combination of characteristics, base acute or obtuse 25

25. Bark of older stems and branches loose, peeling off in long, shreddy pieces; fruit a berry 26

25. Bark of older stems and branches smooth, not peeling off in long, shreddy pieces; fruit various 30

   26.   Corolla 5.0 (rarely 4.0) to 11.0 mm long, regular generally without a saccate base; ovary 4-, loculed, 2 locules with several abortive ovules, 2 locules with 1 fertile ovule; fruit a berry, white; flowers solitary, or in axillary or terminal clusters, not always two on a common peduncle; bundle scars 1, inconspicuous; twigs closely branched, slender. (This genus, *Symphoricarpos* Duhamel., is widely distributed in Colorado with 3 native species occurring in our area. These species are difficult to identify without flowers.) 27

   26.   Corolla 15.0 (rarely 10.0) mm long or longer, more or less irregular, saccate; ovary 2 to 3 loculed, each locule with several ovules; fruit a berry, black, purple, or red in cultivated species; flowers in pairs, rarely 3, on axillary peduncles; bundle scars 3, inconspicuous; twigs not closely branched, medium thickness. (This genus, *Lonicera* L., has 1 native species and several introduced species in our area.) 29

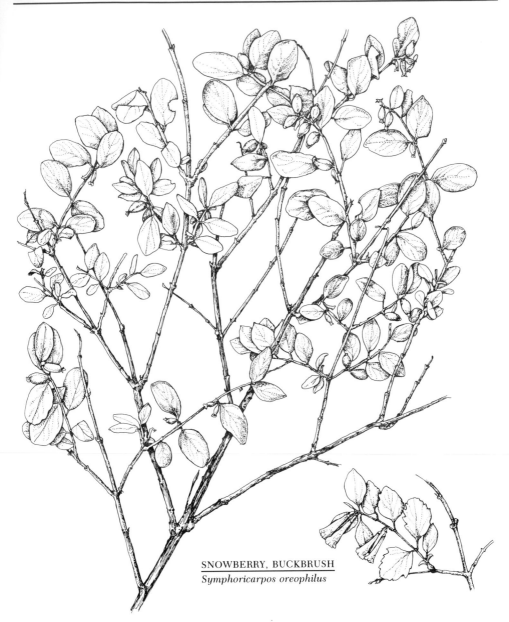

SNOWBERRY, BUCKBRUSH
Symphoricarpos oreophilus

27.   Young twigs glabrous; corolla tubular or funnelform, tube pubescent below insertion of stamens on inside, lobes 1/4 to 1/2 the length of the tube; fruit ovoid to ellipsoid; shrub to 1.5 m tall; occurring at 5,000 to 9,000 ft (1524 to 2743 m).

       SNOWBERRY, BUCKBRUSH, *Symphoricarpos oreophilus* A. Gray
                                                          (Caprifoliaceae)

27.   Young twigs pubescent; corolla companulate to funnelform, tube densely hairy within, lobes 1/2 to as long as or longer than tube 28

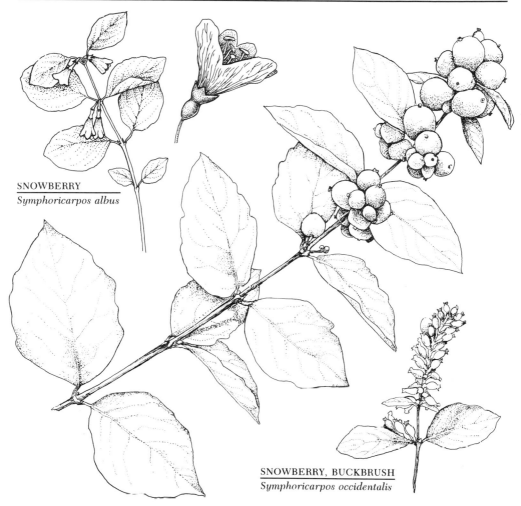

SNOWBERRY
Symphoricarpos albus

SNOWBERRY, BUCKBRUSH
Symphoricarpos occidentalis

28.   Mature leaves less than 5.0 cm long; stamens remaining within corolla; corolla campanulate, sometimes saccate, lobe 1/2 to as long as the tube; inflorescence a few flowered raceme; fruit ovoid, white, smooth, not lustrous; shrub less than 1.0 m tall; occurring on dry rocky soil and gravelly banks.

     SNOWBERRY, BUCKBRUSH, *Symphoricarpos albus* (L.) Blake
                                                       (Caprifoliaceae)

28.   Mature leaves 3.0 to 10.0 cm long; stamens exerted; corolla campanulate or funnelform, lobe equal to or longer than tube; inflorescence a many flowered raceme; fruit globose, greenish-white, occasionally with a few brownish dots on the surface; shrub less than 1.0 m tall; occurring on plains, mesas, and foothills, from 4,000 to 8,500 ft (1219 to 2591 m).

     SNOWBERRY, BUCKBRUSH, *Symphoricarpos occidentalis* Hook.
                                                       (Caprifoliaceae)

BUSH HONEYSUCKLE
Lonicera involucrata

29.   Fruit black or purplish-black, shiny; corolla yellow, sometimes tinged with red, lobes 1/2 as long as tube; peduncles more than 15.0 mm long; mature leaves 5.0 to 15.0 cm long; shrubs native to Colorado; occurring at 7,000 to 11,500 ft (2134 to 3505 m).

BUSH HONEYSUCKLE, *Lonicera involucrata* (Richards.)
Banks ex Spreng.   (Caprifoliaceae)

29.   Fruit red or orange-red; corolla white or, pink, sometimes fading to yellow, lobes equal to or as long as tube; peduncles 5.0 to 15.0 mm long; mature leaves 2.0 to 7.0 cm long; shrubs introduced to Colorado; occurring in lawns, occasionally escaping cultivation.

HONEYSUCKLE, *Lonicera* L.   (Caprifoliaceae)

Two species occur in our area, *Lonicera morrowi* A. Gray and *Lonicera tatarica* L. Generally, *Lonicera morrowi* has a longer peduncle (10.0 to 18.0 mm) and a white, often fading to yellow, corolla; whereas *Lonicera tatarica* has a shorter peduncle (4.0 to 15.0, rarely 18.0, mm) and a white or pink corolla.

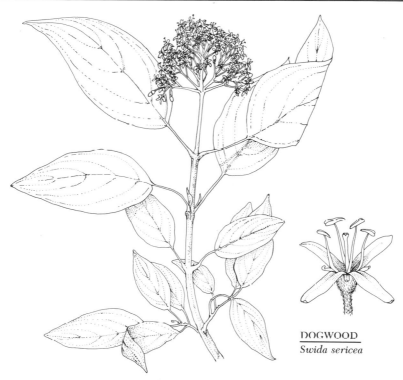

DOGWOOD
Swida sericea

30. Leaves with lateral veins running parallel with the margins to near the apex; branches red-colored; fruit a drupe; common from foothills to subalpine, occasionally cultivated in cities.

DOGWOOD, *Swida sericea* (L.) Holub.   (Cornaceae)
(previously: *Cornus stolonifera* Michx.)

30. Leaves with lateral veins ending near the margin and not running to the apex; branches cream-colored, reddish-brown or gray, never red . 31

31. Leaves 6.0 to 15.0 cm long; flowers in pairs, yellow; fruit a berry, black or purplish; plants native to Colorado; occurring at 7,000 to 11,500 ft (2134 to 3505 m).

BUSH HONEYSUCKLE, *Lonicera involucrata* (Richards.)
Banks ex Spreng.   (Caprifoliaceae)

31. Leaves 3.0 to 6.0 cm long; flowers white to cream-colored; fruit a drupe, small, black at maturity; plants introduced to Colorado; often occurring as lawn hedges, escaping to roadsides and disturbed areas.

PRIVET, *Ligustrum vulgare* L.   (Oleaceae)

32. Petiole bases of opposite leaves not joined by a distinct transverse line or ridge across stem 33

32. Petiole bases of opposite leaves joined by a distinct transverse line or ridge across stem 36

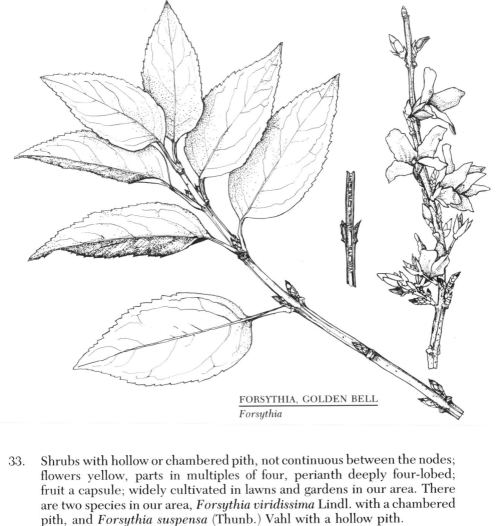

FORSYTHIA, GOLDEN BELL
Forsythia

33. Shrubs with hollow or chambered pith, not continuous between the nodes; flowers yellow, parts in multiples of four, perianth deeply four-lobed; fruit a capsule; widely cultivated in lawns and gardens in our area. There are two species in our area, *Forsythia viridissima* Lindl. with a chambered pith, and *Forsythia suspensa* (Thunb.) Vahl with a hollow pith.

FORSYTHIA, GOLDEN BELL, *Forsythia* Vahl.   (Oleaceae)

33. Shrubs or trees with continuous or spongy pith between the nodes; flowers and fruit various 34

34. Fruit a samara, 11.0 to 25.0 mm long, completely winged; leaf shape orbicular, oval to ovate, margin variable but often widely crenate to undulate; dry canyons in southcentral and southwestern Colorado from 4,000 to 6,000 ft (1219 to 1829 m).

COLORADO ASH, *Fraxinus anomala* Torr. ex S. Wats.   (Oleaceae)

34. Fruit a drupe or a capsule; leaf shape lanceolate to oblanceolate, margin finely serrate or crenate 35

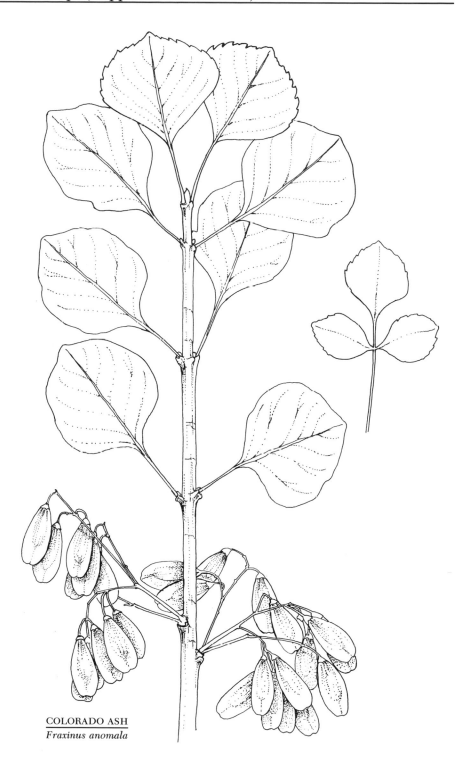

COLORADO ASH
Fraxinus anomala

35.   Mature fruit a drupe, black; flowers inconspicuous, perianth reduced or wanting; native to dry areas from Colorado Springs vicinity south and west; from 4,500 to 6,500 ft (1372 to 1981 m).

FORESTIERA, ADELIA, *Forestiera neomexicana* A. Gray   (Oleaceae)

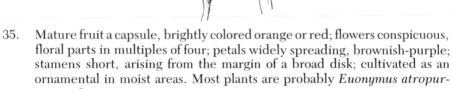

FORESTIERA, ADELIA
Forestiera neomexicana

35.   Mature fruit a capsule, brightly colored orange or red; flowers conspicuous, floral parts in multiples of four; petals widely spreading, brownish-purple; stamens short, arising from the margin of a broad disk; cultivated as an ornamental in moist areas. Most plants are probably *Euonymus atropurpureus* Jacq.

BURNING BUSH, WAHOO, *Euonymus* L.   (Celastraceae)

36.   Buds imbedded under the petiole base, not axillary; leaves often soft-pubescent on lower surface; fruit a capsule 37

36.   Buds not imbedded under the petiole base, but axillary; leaves seldom pubescent on the lower surface; fruit a drupe, sometimes berry-like 38

37.   Leaves with 3 main veins from near the base, often softly pubescent below; young twigs brown to gray, rarely red; sepals 4, rarely 5, lobed; stamens 15 or more. One native species in our area, *Philadelphus microphyllus* A. Gray, but several introduced species are cultivated in lawns and gardens.

MOCKORANGE, *Philadelphus* L.   (Hydrangeaceae)

37.   Leaves pinnately veined with 1 main vein from near the base, whitish-tomentose below; young branches red or reddish brown, bark peeling; sepals 5; petals 5; stamens 10; native to this region; from the foothills to subalpine, 6,000 to 10,000 ft (1829 to 3048 m).

   WAXFLOWER, *Jamesia americana* T. & G.   (Hydrangeaceae)

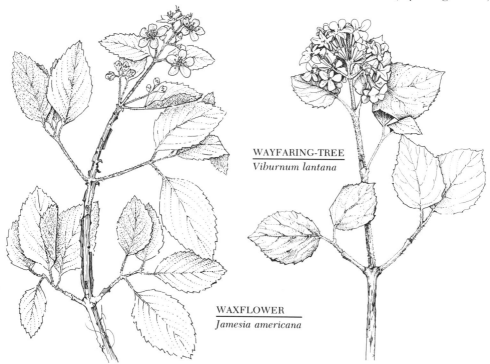

WAYFARING-TREE
Viburnum lantana

WAXFLOWER
Jamesia americana

38.   Flowers and fruit in compound flat-topped or somewhat rounded cymes; corolla white; styles 3 lobed or 3 cleft; fruit a 1-seeded drupe, usually red, blue, or black. (This genus, *Viburnum* L., with three native species is widely cultivated in lawns and gardens in this area.) 39

38.   Flowers in axillary pairs, small clusters, or solitary, if in small terminal clusters then not forming a flat-topped inflorescence; corolla pink or white; styles not branched; fruit a 2-seeded berry-like drupe, white. (This genus, *Symphoricarpos* Duhamel., is widely distributed in Colorado with 3 native species occurring in our area.) 40

39.   Leaves covered on both surfaces with gray stellate hairs, strongly veined; buds naked; introduced to this area, but escaping cultivation.

   WAYFARING-TREE, *Viburnum lantana* L.   (Caprifoliaceae)

39.   Leaves glabrous or with little pubescence, not strongly veined; buds scaly; introduced to this area, but escaping cultivation.

   NANNYBERRY, *Viburnum lentago* L.   (Caprifoliaceae)

(See illustrations for these species of *Symphoricarpos*, pages 24 and 25.)

40.   Young twigs glabrous; corolla tubular or funnelform, tube pubescent below insertion of stamens on inside, lobes 1/4 to 1/2 length of the tube; fruit ovoid to ellipsoid; shrub to 1.5 m tall; occurring from 5,000 to 9,000 ft (1524 to 2743 m).

SNOWBERRY, BUCKBRUSH, *Symphoricarpos oreophilus* A. Gray
(Caprifoliaceae)

40.   Young twigs pubescent; corolla campanulate to funnelform, tube densely hairy within, lobes 1/2 to as long as or longer than tube 41

41.   Mature leaves less than 5.0 cm long; stamens remaining within corolla; corolla campanulate, sometimes saccate, lobe 1/2 to as long as tube; inflorescence in few flowered raceme; fruit ovoid, white, smooth, not lustrous; shrub less than 1.0 m tall; occurring in dry rocky soil and gravelly banks.

SNOWBERRY, BUCKBRUSH, *Symphoricarpos albus* (L.) Blake
(Caprifoliaceae)

41.   Mature leaves 3.0 to 10.0 cm long; stamens exerted; corolla campanulate or funnelform, lobe equal to or longer than tube; inflorescence a many flowered raceme; fruit globose, greenish-white, occasionally with a few brownish dots on the surface; shrub less than 1.0 m tall; occurring on plains, mesas, and foothills, from 4,000 to 8,500 ft (1219 to 2591 m).

SNOWBERRY, BUCKBRUSH, *Symphoricarpos occidentalis* Hook.
(Caprifoliaceae)

KEY III

Compound, Opposite, Broad Leaves

1. Stems climbing, twining, or if erect then plant usually less than 50.0 cm tall; often vines becoming woody with age (In this genus, *Clematis* L., petals are absent and sepals are petaloid.) 2

1. Stems erect, not climbing or twining; trees or shrubs over 50.0 cm tall 7

  2. Sepals white, cream, or yellow and tinged with green; plants dioecious or polygamodioecious 3

  2. Sepals blue to purple or reddish-purple, rarely white; plants with perfect flowers; may appear as an herbaceous shrubs, spreading from woody rhizome 4

3. Sepals white or cream, oblanceolate or oblong, less than 1.0 cm long; leaflets coarsely toothed or lobed to nearly entire, basal leaflet usually the largest; leaves thickish, yellow-green to bright green, pinnately compound; native vines; occurring in thickets over bushes and rocks, along roads, in moist canyons, or on hillsides, 3,000 to 8,500 ft (914 to 2591 m).

WESTERN VIRGIN'S BOWER, *Clematis ligusticifolia* Nutt. ex T. & G.

(Ranunculaceae)

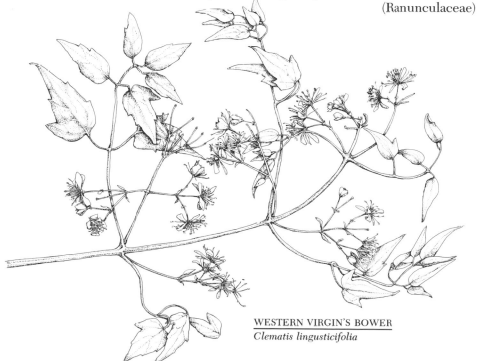

WESTERN VIRGIN'S BOWER
Clematis lingusticifolia

3.   Sepals yellow with greenish tinge, elliptic, over 1.5 cm long; leaflets entire, toothed or lobed, terminal leaflet usually the largest; leaves dull green above, paler below, bi- or triternately compound; introduced vines from Asia, occasionally escaping cultivation, from 6,000 to 8,000 ft (1829 to 2438 m).

ORIENTAL CLEMATIS, *Clematis orientalis* L.   (Ranunculaceae)

4.   Leaves trifoliate, bi- or triternately compound; sepals thin 5

4.   Leaves pinnately dissected or compound; sepals thick; plants not climbing 6

ORIENTAL CLEMATIS
Clematis orientalis

5.   Leaves trifoliate; leaflets 3.0 to 6.0 cm long, entire, toothed or cleft; flowers solitary on terminal bractless peduncles; climbing vines in wooded or open areas, often on talus slopes, 6,000 to 10,000 ft (1829 to 3048 m).

ROCKY MOUNTAIN CLEMATIS, *Clematis columbiana* (Nutt.) T. & G.
(Ranunculaceae)

5.   Leaves bi- or triternate; leaflets usually less than 3 cm long, lobed or incisely 3 to 7 toothed or cleft; flowers solitary or a few together in leaf axils; trailing or climbing vines in thickets or open wooded hillsides, 6,000 to 10,000 ft (1829 to 3048 m). This may be a subspecies of *Clematis columbiana*.

ROCKY MOUNTAIN CLEMATIS, *Clematis pseudoalpina* (Kuntze) A. Nelson
(Ranunculaceae)

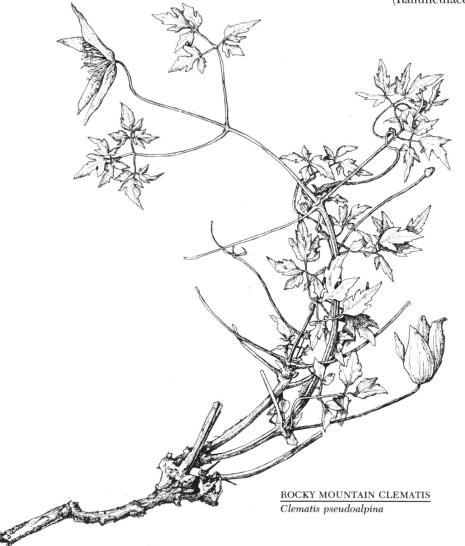

ROCKY MOUNTAIN CLEMATIS
Clematis pseudoalpina

6.   Leaflets 7 to 13, pinnatified into linear or lanceolate segments; stems erect; occurring in grasslands, sagebrush plains, or open ponderosa pine forests, 5,000 to 9,000 ft (1524 to 2743 m).

SUGARBOWLS, *Clematis hirsutissima* Pursh   (Ranunculaceae)

6.   Leaflets 5 to 11, lanceolate to ovate, margins entire; stems somewhat decumbent; plants erect or trailing; occurring in mountainous areas, 6,500 to 8,500 ft (1981 to 2591 m). This species is sometimes considered a variety of *Clematis hirsutissima*.

SUGARBOWLS, *Clematis scottii* Porter & Coulter   (Ranunculaceae)

ELDERBERRY
Sambucus canadensis

8.   Pith large, comprising most of the stem; bark with large, raised, corky lenticels; fruit a berry 9

8.   Pith small, comprising less than 25 percent of the stem; bark lacking lenticels, or if present, not conspicuous; fruit a samara 10

9.   Inflorescence flat-topped or umbrella-shaped, axis seldom extending beyond the lowest branches; berries black; common along creeks and roadsides, plains to foothills; probably escaping cultivation.

ELDERBERRY, *Sambucus canadensis* L.   (Caprifoliaceae)

9.   Inflorescence short-pyramidal, axis extending beyond the lowest branches; berries orange-red to red, sometimes yellowish; common along streams and on moist slopes, from 8,000 to 12,000 ft (2438 to 3658 m).

REDBERRIED ELDER, *Sambucus racemosa* L.   (Caprifoliaceae)

REDBERRIED ELDER
Sambucus racemosa

10. Leaflets 3 to 7, lobed or coarsely serrate above the middle, light yellow-green above, pale below; twigs often glaucous; buds light green; samaras paired, curved; commonly escaping cultivation.

BOX ELDER, *Acer negundo* L.   (Aceraceae)

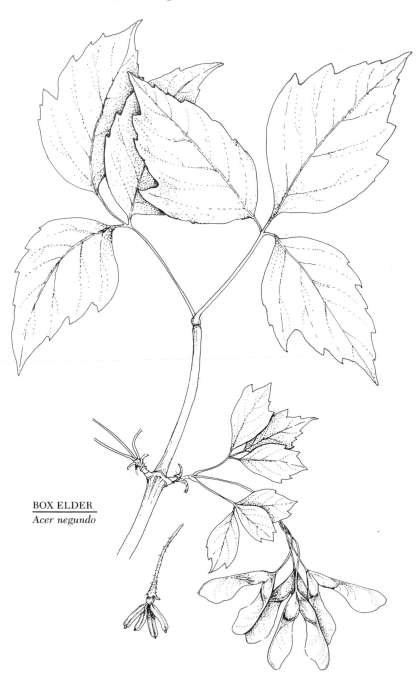

BOX ELDER
Acer negundo

10. Leaflets 5 to 9, entire or finely serrate, dark green above, pale below; twigs not glaucous; buds brown or black; samaras solitary, linear to spatulate, symmetrical; common tree of lawns and gardens, escaping cultivation.

GREEN ASH, *Fraxinus pennsylvanica* Marsh.   (Oleaceae)

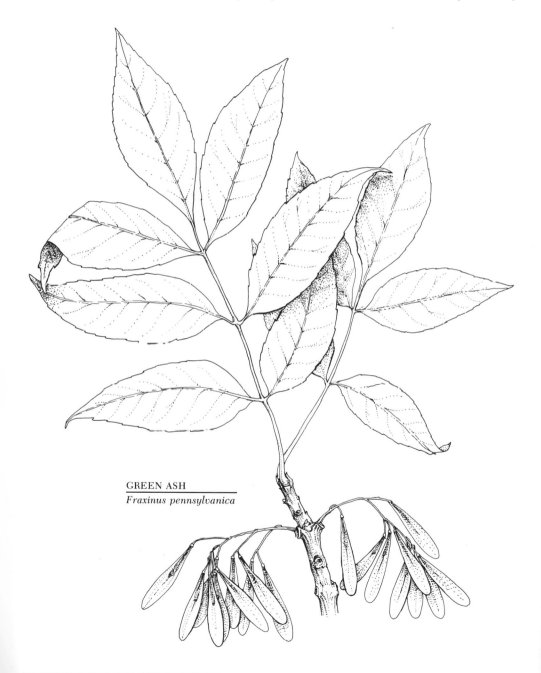

GREEN ASH
Fraxinus pennsylvanica

11.   Leaves palmately compound with more than 3 leaflets; leaflets obovate to oblanceolate, margins minutely serrate, teeth less than 1.0 mm long; fruit a globose capsule forming a rusty-brown, spiny hull, 3.0 to 4.50 cm in diameter; cultivated tree in our area.

      HORSE CHESTNUT, BUCKEYE, *Aesculus glabra* Willd.   (Hippocastanaceae)

HORSE CHESTNUT, BUCKEYE
Aesculus glabra

11.   Leaves trifoliate, if more than 3 leaflets then pinnately compound; leaflet ovate, margins conspicuously serrate, teeth to 8.0 mm long; fruit a paired samara 12

     12.   Leaves trifoliate, averaging less than 6 cm in length, lower surface lacking pubescence along veins; terminal leaflet base attenuate; new stems red to brown; twigs slender, weak; common along streams and in canyons; foothills to montane. (See illustration, page 14.)

        MOUNTAIN MAPLE, *Acer glabrum* Torr.   (Aceraceae)

     12.   Leaves trifoliate or pinnately compound, averaging more than 6.0 cm in length, lower surface pubescent along veins; terminal leaflet base broadly cuneate or rounded; new stems green to blue or gray, often glaucous; twigs stout; common on stream banks; plains to foothills, and introduced as shade tree in lawns.

        BOX ELDER, *Acer negundo* L.   (Aceraceae)

KEY IV

Simple, Alternate, Broad Leaves

1.   Leaves lobed or deeply notched 2

1.   Leaves not lobed 28

    2.   Stems climbing and twining, forming vines; leaves usually palmately lobed and up to 20.0 cm in width; common in lower canyons and foothills, along streambanks, road-sides and edges of woods.

       WILD GRAPE, *Vitis riparia* Michx.   (Vitaceae)

    2.   Stems forming trees and shrubs, never forming climbing or twining vines; leaves variously lobed 3

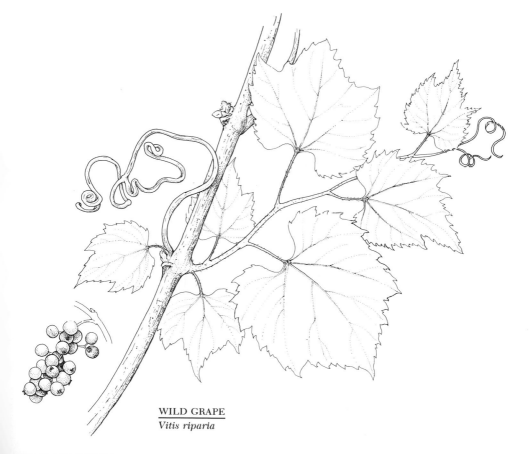

WILD GRAPE
Vitis riparia

3.   Leaves pinnately lobed, with one main vein (midrib) from the base 4

3.   Leaves palmately lobed, with more than one main vein (midrib) from near the base 10

     4.   Leaf margins ranging from serrate to crenate; leaf bases ranging from cordate to oblique; fruit a cylindric multiple, consisting of many small drupelets; commonly cultivated, usually occurring in the open or prairie hills, in rocky ground.

         WHITE MULBERRY, RED MULBERRY, *Morus alba* L.   (Moraceae)

     4.   Leaf margins entire 5

WHITE MULBERRY,
RED MULBERRY
Morus alba

5.   Petioles absent or not distinct, reduced in length or absent; leaf margins revolute; achenes plumose; older bark shredding with age 6

5.   Petioles present but not always distinct; leaf margins flat; older bark not shredding with age 7

6.   Leaves in clusters or fascicles, pubescent, villous or glabrous above with age, rusty-scaly below; stipules present; achenes 5 to 10, with persistent plumose styles; shrubs 0.5 to 1.5 m tall; occurring on hills, slopes,.

   APACHE PLUME, *Fallugia paradoxa* (D. Don) Endl.   (Rosaceae)

6.   Leaves distributed along the stems, not in clusters, glandular-punctate above, whitish-tomentose below; stipules absent; achenes numerous, with persistent plumose styles; shrubs to 3.5 m tall; occurring on hills and slopes, generally in southwest Colorado, 4,500 to 7,500 ft (1372 to 2286 m).

   CLIFFROSE, *Cowania mexicana* Don   (Rosaceae)

APACHE PLUME
Fallugia paradoxa

CLIFFROSE
Cowania mexicana

7. Basal leaves present; mature leaves deeply divided or dissected to the midrib, leaf segments linear to linear-filiform or oblong, with an aroma of sage; stipules absent; flowers in heads on leafy panicles or racemes; fruit an achene; shrubs, mostly herbaceous, usually less than 1.0 m tall 8

7. Basal leaves absent; mature leaves shallowly lobed or divided to deeply dissected to the midrib, leaf segments variously shaped, but never linear, without an aroma of sage; stipules present, often early deciduous; flowers monecious, staminate flowers in catkins, pistillate flowers solitary, in pairs, or clusters; fruit an acorn; shrubs or trees usually over 1.0 m tall (genus *Quercus* L.) 9

PASTURE SAGEBRUSH
Artemesia frigida

8.   Leaf segments narrowly linear and finely dissected, less than 1.0
      mm wide; leaves along stems less than 2.5 cm long; plants 10.0 to
      50.0 cm tall; native to Colorado; occurring on dry plains, hills, and
      mountains, especially in the western half of Colorado, 4,500 to 10,000
      ft (1372 to 3048 m).

      PASTURE SAGEBRUSH, *Artemesia frigida* Willd.   (Asteraceae)

8.   Leaf segments lanceolate, 1.0 to 2.0 mm wide; leaves along stems
      more than 3.0 cm long; plants usually over 50.0 cm tall; introduced
      to Colorado; occurring in waste places and near dwellings.

      INTRODUCED SAGE, *Artemesia absinthium* L.   (Asteraceae)

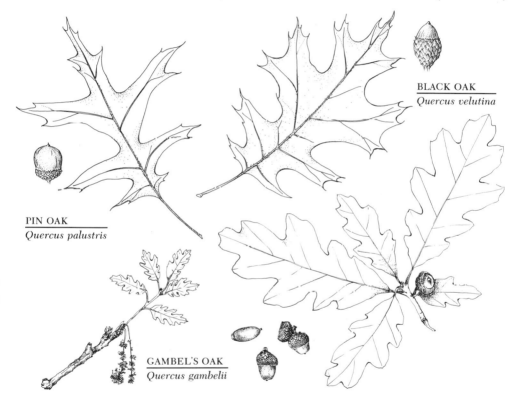

BLACK OAK
Quercus velutina

PIN OAK
Quercus palustris

GAMBEL'S OAK
Quercus gambelii

9.   Leaves oblong or ovate, lobed or divided, lobes acute rounded or obtuse,
      deciduous shedding in fall; shrubs or small trees; native, occurring on dry
      foothills, canyon walls, stream margins, 4,000 to 8,500 ft (1219 to 2591 m).

      GAMBEL'S OAK, *Quercus gambelii* Nutt.   (Fagaceae)

9.   Leaves oblong, ovate to obovate, deeply lobed and dissected, spine-tipped
      to aristate lobes, deciduous, often persisting until spring; introduced or
      cultivated trees. Two introduced oaks can be found in this area, **PIN
      OAK,** *Quercus palustris* Muenchh. and **BLACK OAK,** *Quercus velutina*
      Lam.

10. Stems or branches with spines or thorns 11

10. Stems or branches without spines or thorns 15

11. Spines 1.5 cm or more long, glaucous; leaves 5.0 to 20.0 mm long including petiole, villous; petioles indistinct; stems white tomemtose; fruit an achene; rounded shrubs 5.0 to 50.0 cm tall; occurring on dry plains and slopes of western Colorado.

SPINY SAGE, *Artemisia spinescens* D.C. Eaton   (Asteraceae)

11. Spines less than 1.5 cm long, glossy; leaves 1.0 to 3.0 cm long not including petioles, glabrous to glandular-pubescent; petioles distinct; stems bristly or smooth; fruit a berry (genus *Ribes* L.) 12

   12. Younger twigs with bristles in the internodes; branches often drooping; flower calyx tube not over 2.0 mm long; fruit with gland-tipped bristles; species of wet forests, meadows, and along streams 13

   12. Younger twigs without bristles in the internodes; branches often erect; flower calyx tube over 2.0 mm long; fruit glabrous to rarely gland-tipped, hispid or bristly 14

13. Spines 1 at each node; leaf blades glabrous; mature fruit purple to black; shrubs with ascending or drooping stems, usually less than 100.0 cm tall; occurring in wet meadows, in the montane to subalpine regions of northern counties in Colorado, 8,000 to 10,000 ft (2438 to 3048 m).

PRICKLY CURRANT, *Ribes lacustre* (Pers.) Poir   (Grossulariaceae)

13. Spines 3 at a node; leaf blades pubescent to glandular pubescent; mature fruit red; low shrubs, freely branching, 30.0 to 60.0 cm tall; occurring in wet forests in the subalpine region, especially in western Colorado, 7,500 to 11,500 ft (2286 to 3658 m).

ALPINE PRICKLY CURRANT, *Ribes montigenum* McClatchie
(Grossulariaceae)

   14. Style glabrous; sepals erect; petals narrow and oblong; leaves 0.5 to 2.5 cm wide, usually 3 lobed or dentate; erect shrubs 50.0 to 200.0 cm tall; occurring in the mountains, often in dry places, 5,500 to 12,000 ft (1676 to 3658 m). *Ribes leptanthum* A. Gray is difficult to distinguish from *Ribes inerme* Rybd. without flowers.

   WESTERN GOOSEBERRY, *Ribes leptanthum* A. Gray   (Grossulariaceae)

   14. Style pilose-pubescent; sepals reflexed; petals broader, shorter than the sepals; leaves 1.0 to 6.0 cm wide, 3 to 5 lobed or dentate; erect shrubs about 100.0 cm tall; occurring in the mountains, 5,000 to 11,000 ft (1524 to 3353 m).

   COMMON GOOSEBERRY, *Ribes inerme* Rydb.   (Grossulariaceae)

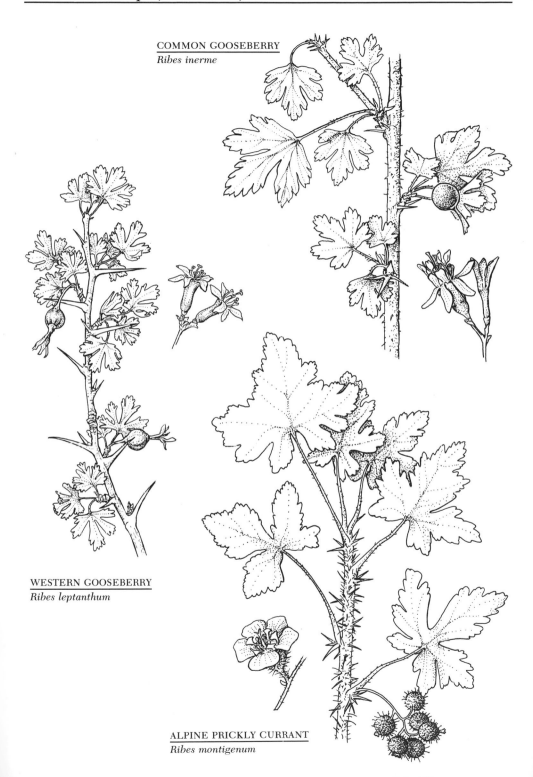

COMMON GOOSEBERRY
Ribes inerme

WESTERN GOOSEBERRY
Ribes leptanthum

ALPINE PRICKLY CURRANT
Ribes montigenum

BOULDER RASPBERRY
Rubus deliciosus

17.   Petioles glabrous to only slightly pubescent; leaf blades ovate to suborbicular, usually longer than broad; stipules 2.0 to 3.0 mm long; flowers 15 to 25 in a corymb, 1 to 10 pistils per flower; fruit an inflated capsule or follicle 19

   18.   Mature leaves 3.0 to 6.0 cm wide, lobes rounded; flowers solitary; shrubs to 1.5 m tall; occurring in foothills and canyons, often in rocky ground, 4,500 to 9,000 ft (1372 to 2743 m).

   BOULDER RASPBERRY, *Rubus deliciosus* James   (Rosaceae)

   18.   Mature leaves 8.0 to 30.0 cm wide, lobes acute; flowers 2 to 9 in cymose clusters; shrubs 1.0 to 2.0 m tall; occurring in open woods and slopes, foothills to subalpine, 7,000 to 10,000 ft (2134 to 3048 m).

   THIMBLEBERRY, *Rubus parviflorus* Torr.   (Rosaceae)

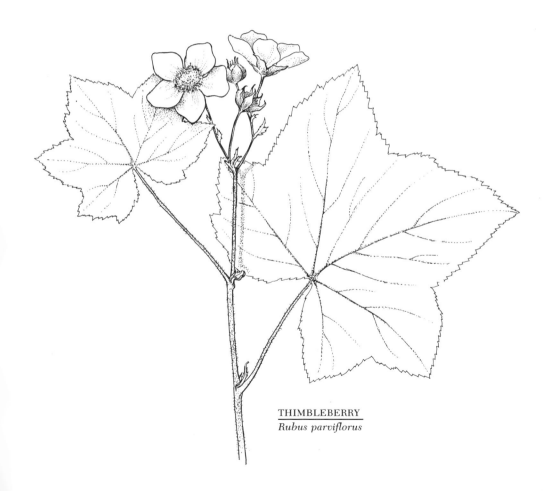

THIMBLEBERRY
Rubus parviflorus

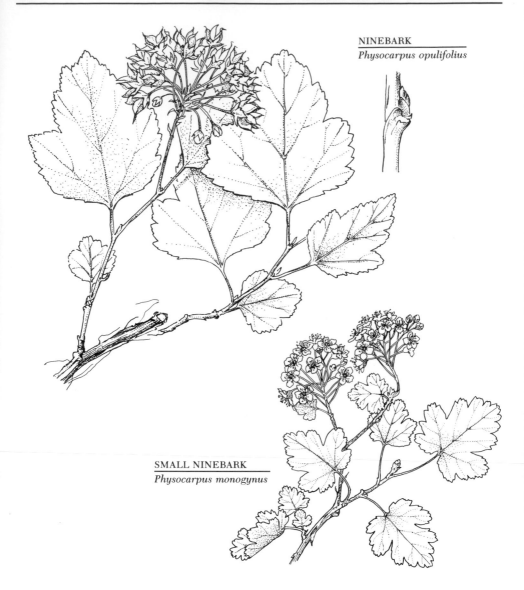

SMALL NINEBARK
Physocarpus monogynus

19.   Leaf bases acute; blades 3.0 to 8.0 cm long, usually 3 lobed; fruit 1.0 cm or less in length consisting of 3 to 5 follicles; shrubs 100.0 cm or less tall; occurring in the foothills, on moist rocky or sandy stream banks, 4,000 to 7,000 ft (1219 to 2134 m).

      NINEBARK, *Physocarpus opulifolius* (L.) Maxim.   (Rosaceae)

19.   Leaf bases truncate to cordate; blades 2.0 to 3.0 cm long, usually 5 lobed; fruit 5.0 mm or less in length, consisting of a 2 or 3 lobed capsule; shrubs 50.0 to 200.0 cm tall; common in dry and open woods, foothills to subalpine, 6,000 to 10,000 ft (1829 to 3048 m).

      SMALL NINEBARK, *Physocarpus monogynus* (Torr.) Coult.   (Rosaceae)

20.   Leaves 1.0 to 3.5 cm wide, 2.0 to 2.5 cm long, shallowly lobed, margins crenate, often clustered on short spurs; leaf scars narrow, extending half way around the stem; buds often with a clear liquid resin along margins; flower calyx tube cylindrical, 3 to 4 times longer than wide; fruit a berry, red, covered with stalked glands; shrub 50.0 to 200.0 cm tall; common on dry slopes, plains to montane, 4,000 to 11,000 ft (1219 to 3353 m).

   WAX CURRANT, *Ribes cereum* Dougl.   (Grossulariaceae)

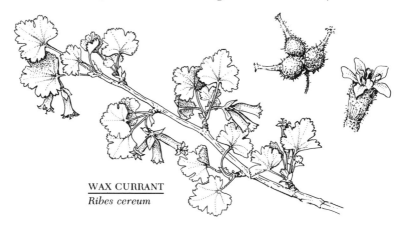

WAX CURRANT
Ribes cereum

20.   Leaves over 4.0 cm wide, distinctly 3 to 5 lobed, margins acutely serrate to dentate, distributed along stem, not clustered in spurs; leaf scars V-shaped or narrow crescent-shaped; buds not forming a clear liquid resin along margins; fruit a berry, dark red to purple-black 21

21. Calyx tube becoming saucer-shaped or bowl-shaped above ovary, less than 2.0 mm long; leaves generally 5 lobed, bases distinctly cordate, margins doubly serrate; fruit black, with glandular hairs 22

21. Calyx tube cylindrical above ovary, 3.0 mm long or longer; leaves generally 3 lobed, bases cuneate to truncate to subcordate, margins serrate or dentate; fruit dark red to purple or nearly black, glabrous 23

   22.   Stems stout, not trailing, 1.0 to 1.5 m tall; calyx lobes linear to oblong-ovate; flower clusters arise from the buds of the current year's growth; berry glandular-bristly; species of the mountains in the western half of Colorado, often in partial shade, 6,500 to 11,500 ft (1981 to 3505 m).

   WESTERN CURRANT, *Ribes wolfii* Rothrock   (Grossulariaceae)

   22.   Stems weak, trailing or prostrate; calyx lobes ovate, about as wide as long; flower clusters arise from the buds of the previous year's growth; berry sparingly glandular-hairy; species of the mountains in the western half of Colorado, 8,000 to 11,500 ft (2438 to 3505 m).

   COLORADO CURRANT, *Ribes coloradense* Coville   (Grossulariaceae)

23.   Leaves 4.0 to 9.0 cm wide, lobes acute, margins serrate or doubly serrate; leaf surface pubescent on veins, covered with many sessile yellow or orange glands; petioles 4.0 cm or more long; calyx tube 3.0 to 4.0 mm long; flowers greenish-yellow to white, in drooping racemes; rare in natural habitats, occurring in moist wooded areas; commonly cultivated.

BLACK CURRANT, *Ribes americanum* Mill.   (Grossulariaceae)

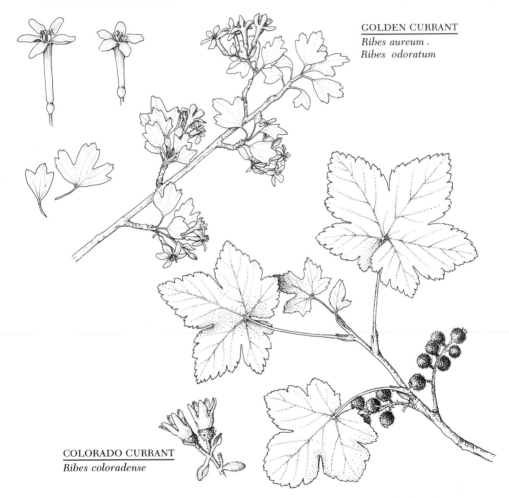

GOLDEN CURRANT
Ribes aureum ,
Ribes odoratum

COLORADO CURRANT
Ribes coloradense

23.   Leaves 4.0 cm or less wide, lobes subobtuse, margins coarsely dentate, leaf surface glabrous on veins, covered with very few pale glands; petioles less than 4.0 cm long; calyx tube 5.0 to 10.0 mm long; flowers bright yellow, solitary or in erect racemes; common, plains to foothills and mountains, along roadsides and streams, 3,500 to 8,000 ft (1067 to 2438 m).

GOLDEN CURRANT, *Ribes aureum* Pursh   (Grossulariaceae)

[GOLDEN CURRANT, *Ribes odoratum* Wendl. will key to this point. This rather rare species occurs on the plains and is distinguished by a hypanthium (calyx tube) of more than 10.0 mm in length.]

24.   Mature plants more than 4.0 m tall, trees; leaves over 4.0 cm wide; bark peeling into short thin flakes; species introduced and commonly escaping cultivation 25

24.   Mature plants less than 4.0 m tall, shrubs; leaves less than 4.0 cm wide; bark not peeling; species native to high plains and prairies in dry habitats 26

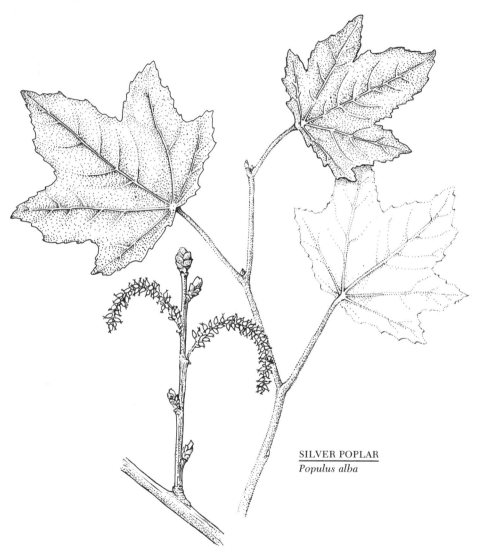

SILVER POPLAR
Populus alba

25.   Petiole 2.0 to 4.0 cm long, flattened, base not hollow; leaves 4.0 to 8.0 cm wide with 3 to 5 shallow lobes or undulate margins, lower surface densely white tomemtose; fruit a pendulous catkin.

SILVER POPLAR, *Populus alba* L.   (Salicaceae)

25. Petiole 5.0 to 7.0 cm long, not flattened, base hollow forming a hood over the lateral bud; leaves 8.0 to 20.0 cm wide with 3 to 5 coarsely toothed lobes, lower surface pale green, glabrous with pubescent midrib and veins; fruit a persistent suspended ball of hairy achenes.

SYCAMORE, *Platanus occidentalis* L.　　　　　　　　　　　(Platanaceae)

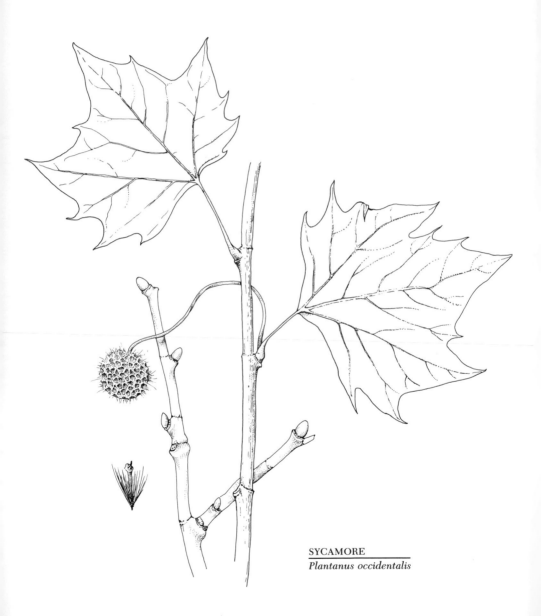

SYCAMORE
Plantanus occidentalis

26.   Leaves thread-like, 3.0 to 8.0 cm long, lobed in filiform divisions, lobes seldom over 0.5 mm wide; twigs slender, smooth, reddish; shrubs 30.0 to 150.0 cm tall; common to sandy habitats on the plains, scattered throughout eastern half of Colorado, 3,500 to 5,000 ft (1067 to 1524 m).

THREAD-LEAVED SAGEBRUSH, WIZENED SAGE,
Artemesia filifolia Torr.   (Asteraceae)

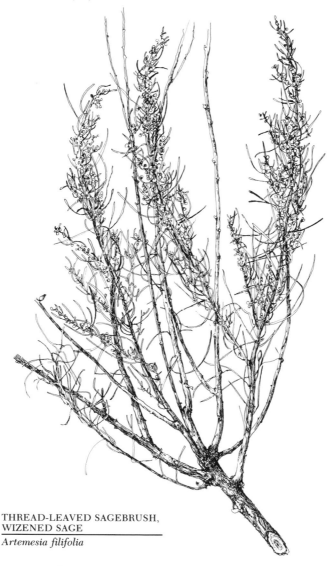

THREAD-LEAVED SAGEBRUSH,
WIZENED SAGE
Artemesia filifolia

26.   Leaves oblanceolate, 0.5 to 3.5 cm long, 3 lobed or 3-toothed at the apex; leaves or their divisions broader, usually over 0.5 mm in width; twigs stout, rough or canescent, grayish or silvery; plants common throughout western Colorado, 4,500 to 8,500 ft (1372 to 2591 m) 27

27. Leaf margins revolute; leaves crowded, appearing to be in clusters, distinctly 3-cleft, lobes simple; upper leaf surface dark green, glabrous to slightly tomemtose; flowers solitary, terminating short branches; fruit an achene covered with short soft hairs; shrubs to 300.0 cm tall; south-facing slopes in western Colorado from 4,500 to 8,000 ft (1370 to 2400 m).

BITTERBRUSH, ANTELOPE-BUSH, *Purshia tridentata* (Pursh) DC.

(Rosaceae)

BITTERBRUSH, ANTELOPE-BUSH
Purshia tridentata

27. Leaf margins flat; leaves distributed singly along stems, shallowly 3-cleft to nearly entire, lobes may be again divided to toothed; upper leaf surface silvery-canescent; flowering heads few to many in spikes, panicles, or racemes; fruit an achene covered with minute granules; shrubs from 10.0 to 400.0 cm tall, common on the western slope from 7,000 to 8,000 ft (2100 to 2400 m).

BIG SAGEBRUSH, WORMWOOD, *Artemisia tridentata* Nutt.   (Asteraceae)

(*Artemesia bigelovii* A. Gray may key to this point. The leaves of *A. bigelovii* are not as deeply toothed or notched as they are in A. tridentata. *A. bigelovii* is less common and more woody than *A. tridentata*.)

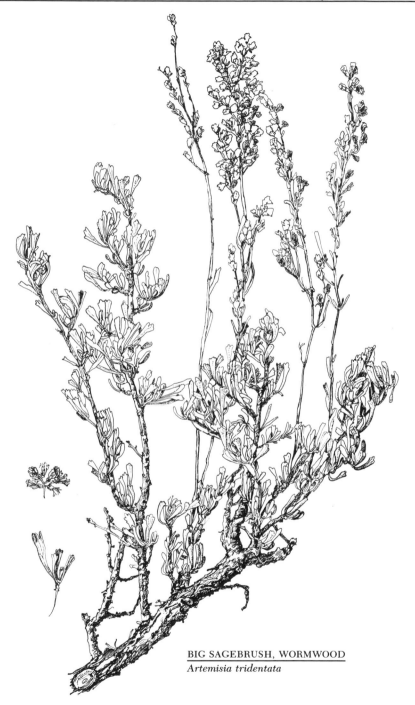

BIG SAGEBRUSH, WORMWOOD
Artemisia tridentata

28.	Stems climbing and twining, forming woody vines	29
28.	Stems forming trees or shrubs, shrubs may be low, but never forming climbing or twining vines	30

29. Margins entire; leaves with 5 to 9 parallel veins from the base, blade ovate to rotund, base cordate to truncate; petioles with a pair of coiled tendrils at the base; stems herbaceous, becoming woody with age; flowers in umbels, greenish, sweet scented; fruit a berry in erect cluster, blue-black, thick; climbing vines occurring in woods and margins of clearings; in central Colorado from 4,500 to 7,000 ft (1370 to 2100 m).

CARRION FLOWER, GREENBRIER, *Smilax lasioneuron* Hook.

(Smilacaceae)

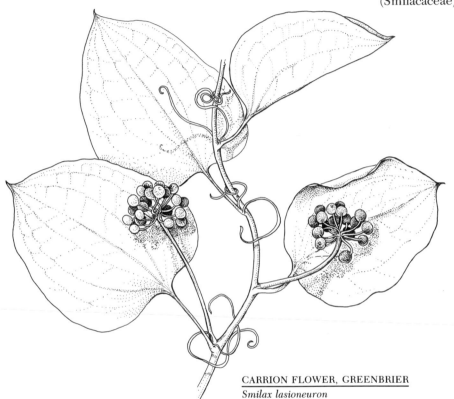

CARRION FLOWER, GREENBRIER
Smilax lasioneuron

29. Margins serrulate; leaves with one main vein (midrib) from the base, blades elliptic to oblong, base tapering to a point; petioles without a pair of tendrils at the base; stems woody throughout; flowers in panicles, yellowish, not sweet or carrion-scented; fruit a capsule in pendulous clusters, bright orange, glandular, wrinkled; twining vines to 12.0 m long, sprawling over bushes or fences, occurring along woods, bluffs, fence-rows, and creek banks; introduced in this region.

BITTERSWEET, *Celastrus scandens* L. (Celastraceae)

31. Stems or branches with spines or thorns, stems sometimes becoming sharp-pointed into thorns or spines (The genus, *Sarcobatus* Nees. may have weak spines.) 32

31. Stems or branches without spines or thorns 40

    32. Mature leaves 4.0 to 12.0 cm long; shrubs or trees 3.0 to 7.0 m tall; mature fruit a dry, scaly drupe 33

    32. Mature leaves less than 4.0 cm long; shrubs to 3.0 m tall 34

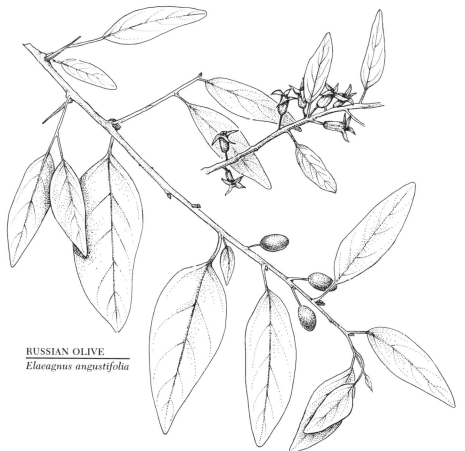

RUSSIAN OLIVE
Elaeagnus angustifolia

33. Mature leaves oblong-lanceolate, less than 2.0 cm wide; young branches silvery scaly; a cultivated tree often escaping cultivation.

RUSSIAN OLIVE, *Elaeagnus angustifolia* L.   (Elaeagnaceae)

33. Mature leaves elliptic to oblong ovate, more than 2.0 cm wide; young branches brown to rusty scaly; a native plant in central Canada and several northern states; often cultivated in Colorado.

SILVERBERRY, *Elaeagnus commutata* Bernh.   (Elaeagnaceae)

34.   Leaves with 3 main veins from near the base; blade distinct from
       petiole; petiole brown, 2.0 to 3.0 mm long; stems covered with
       blister-like glands; flowers white in umbel-like clusters terminating
       the main stems or branches; fruit a capsule with 3 lobes, each lobe
       containing a nutlet-like seed; low shrub 30.0 to 80.0 cm tall; occurring
       in open valleys, hill-sides, and woods, usually in gravelly soil; west-
       ern two-thirds of Colorado from 5,500 to 9,000 ft (1676 to 2743m).

NEW JERSEY TEA, BUCKBRUSH, *Ceanothus fendleri* A. Gray
                                                      (Rhamnaceae)

BUCKBRUSH
Ceanothus fendleri

34.   Leaves with 1 main vein (midrib) from near the base, blade sessile
       on stem, or tapering into an indistinct petiole; petiole, if present,
       similar in color and texture to the blade 35

35. Leaves in fascicles or clusters at the nodes, margins entire or occasionally
     finely dentate; spines present at the nodes below the leaf clusters; flowers
     perfect; fruit a berry 36

35. Leaves distributed singly along the stems, margins entire; spines present
     at the internodes or at end of stem or branch; flowers imperfect; fruit a
     utricle 38

36. Spines 3-parted at the nodes; leaf margins entire to finely dentate; flowers in panicles of 6 to 10; shrubs 0.5 to 1.0 m tall; coming into our area from the Southwest, 5,400 to 8,500 ft (1646 to 2591 m).

BARBERRY, *Berberis fendleri* A. Gray   (Berberidaceae)

36. Spines one at each node; leaf margins entire; leaves in new growth regions may be alternate; flowers solitary, in clusters or small umbels of 2 to 4 37

37. Shrubs cultivated, commonly used for hedges in this area; flowers solitary or in small umbels of 2 to 4; fruit a berry; native of Japan.

JAPANESE BARBERRY, *Berberis thunbergii* DC.   (Berberidaceae)

JAPANESE BARBERRY
Berberis thunbergii

BARBERRY
Berberis fendleri

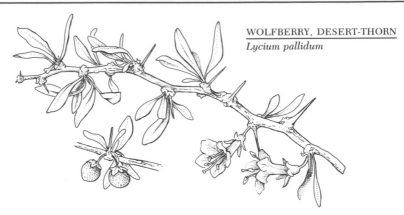

WOLFBERRY, DESERT-THORN
Lycium pallidum

37. Shrubs native, on dry hills and on the plains in southern Colorado; corolla green, tinged with purple, tubular and funnelform, 14.0 to 20.0 mm long; fruit a glaucous red berry; occuring from 4,500 to 7,000 ft (1372 to 2134 m).

WOLFBERRY, DESERT-THORN, *Lycium pallidum* Miers.   (Solanaceae)

38. Leaves narrowly linear, circular in cross- section, less than 2.0 mm wide; twigs with a ridge extending down from the leaf scar; staminate flowers in catkinlike spikes terminating the branches, without a perianth but subtended by peltate bracts; pistillate flowers with a perianth that develops horizonal wings in fruit; occurring in dry alkaline soils south of Colorado Springs, from 4,500 to 8,500 ft (1372 to 2591 m). (See illustration, page 20.)

GREASEWOOD, *Sarcobatus vermiculatus* (Hook.) Torr.
(Chenopodiaceae)

38. Leaves oblanceolate or orbicular ovate, more than 2.0 mm wide; twigs without a ridge extending down from the leaf scar; staminate flowers with a perianth, but lacking bracts; pistillate flowers lacking a definite perianth, but enclosed by 2 accrescent bracts 39

39. Leaves oblanceolate, 4 times longer than wide, sessile, on a short spur which bends around the bud; shrubs 20.0 to 100.0 cm tall; occurring on dry plains and slopes in semi-arid habitats, from 4,500 to 7,500 ft (1372 to 2286 m).

HOP SAGE, *Grayia spinosa* (Hook.) Moq.   (Chenopodiaceae)

39. Leaves orbicular-ovate, about as wide as long, petiolate, not on a short spur bending around the bud; shrubs 20.0 to 100.0 cm tall; occurring on dry plains and slopes in semiarid habitats, 4,500 to 7,500 ft (1372 to 2286 m).

SPINY SALTBUSH, *Atriplex confertifolia* (Torr. & Fremont) S. Wats.
(Chenopodiaceae)

40. Mature leaves lacking petioles, sessile, usually clasping the stem 41

40. Mature leaves with petioles at least 1.5 mm long 61

HOP SAGE
Grayia spinosa

SPINY SALTBUSH
Atriplex confertifolia

41.   Leaves less than 5.0 mm long, bluish-green in color, scale-like, overlapping, leaf base clasping the stem; dense shrub to 5.0 m with slender, flexible, reddish branches; species escapes cultivation to sandy, moist soil along streams and low undrained areas. This species is often confused with the junipers which usually occur on dry and rocky slopes and ridges.

       TAMARISK, SALT CEDAR, *Tamarix pentandra* Pall.   (Tamaricaceae)

41.   Leaves more than 5.0 mm long, not scale-like and not overlapping 42

TAMARISK, SALT CEDAR
Tamarix pentandra

    42.   Leaves 40.0 to 75.0 cm long from a dense basal cluster, rigid with pointed tips, commonly with threadlike fibers along the margins, veins parallel; caudex very short to almost entirely underground, usually hidden by old and dead leaves drooping at the base; flowers 5.0 to 15.0 cm long, campanulate, in terminal racemes or panicles 30.0 to 150.0 cm long; fruit a cylindric capsule, 5.0 to 20.0 cm long; plants occurring in dry, well-drained sandy or limestone soils in open areas, plains to foothills, 4,000 to 8,500 ft (1219 to 2591 m) 43

    42.   Leaves less than 8.0 cm long, flexible, veins netted, attached to stems, or if basal then leaves herbaceous and highly dissected 44

43.   Leaves usually 3.0 cm or more wide; fruit 15.0 to 20.0 cm long, fleshy, berry-like, indehiscent, not opening by pores or slits, pendulous; root system a cluster of fleshy roots close to the caudex; species usually occurring on mesas and low hills in southwestern Colorado.

INDIAN BANANA, *Yucca baccata* Torr.   (Agavaceae)

43.   Leaves usually 1.0 cm or less wide; fruit 5.0 to 8.0 cm long, dry, opening by pores or slits to release seeds, erect; root system a rope-like root going straight down 0.3 to 1.0 m which joins on a horizontal, fleshy storage root; species usually occurring on the plains and into the foothills of the eastern slope.

SOAPWEED, SPANISH BAYONET, *Yucca glauca* Nutt.   (Agavaceae)

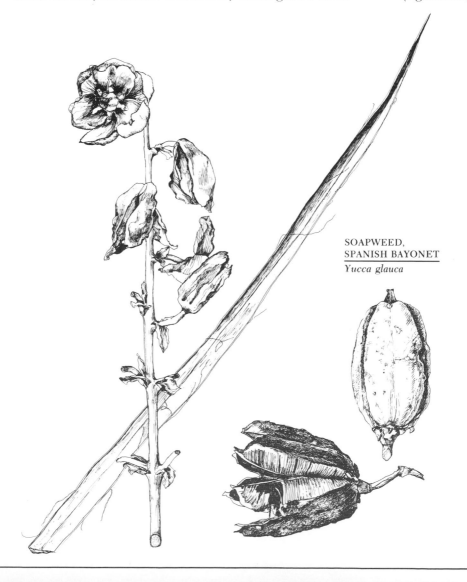

SOAPWEED,
SPANISH BAYONET
Yucca glauca

44.   Flowers solitary, in panicles, or in terminal spikes, if in heads then surrounded by an involucre of bracts 4.0 to 5.0 mm long; leaves linear-oblong, pubescent; commonly a western species 45

44.   Flowers in heads, surrounded by involucre of bracts of various lengths; heads usually in terminal cymes at the tips of the branches, or solitary from a basal rosette of leaves 49

45.   Entire plant dense scurfy or mealy, whitish; flowers unisexual; staminate flowers sessile, in dense clusters on terminal spikes that tower over the bulk of the stems; pistillate flowers solitary, a few together, or in spikes and panicles; fruit a utricle; species common to dry alkaline soils 46

45.   Entire plant neither dense scurfy nor white, but leaves and/or twigs closely tomentose or pubescent; flowers perfect, in tiny heads on loose terminal panicles, or solitary in leaf axils; fruit an achene 47

46.   Bracts of pistillate flowers without 4 conspicuous wings, whole bract 4.0 to 6.0 mm long, obovate or fan-shaped; leaves linear, oblong or linear-spatulate, 0.5 to 2.5 cm long; plants less than 20.0 cm tall, woody at base, forming dense and leafy mats; occurring on dry alkaline flats, plains, or valleys in western Colorado, 4,500 to 8000 ft (1372 to 2438 m).

     WESTERN SALTBUSH, *Atriplex corrugata* S. Wats.   (Chenopodiaceae)

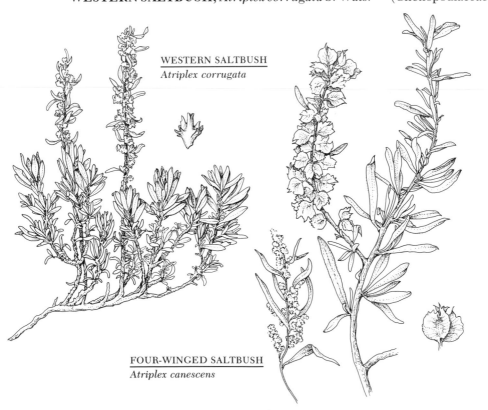

WESTERN SALTBUSH
Atriplex corrugata

FOUR-WINGED SALTBUSH
Atriplex canescens

46.   Bracts of pistillate flowers with 4 conspicuous wings, whole bract 4.0 to 15.0 mm long; leaves linear, oblong to elliptic or spatulate, 1.0 to 5.0 cm long; shrubs 20.0 to 250.0 cm tall, erect, woody throughout; occurring on dry alkaline soils, sandy deserts, and grassy uplands; scattered over the state, 4,000 to 8,000 ft (1219 to 2438 m).

FOUR-WINGED SALTBUSH, *Atriplex canescens (Pursh)* Nutt.

(Chenopodiaceae)

47.   Mature leaves 4.0 to 9.0 cm long, about 10 to 15 times as long as wide, margins flat, surfaces covered with straight appressed hairs attached near the middle; leaves distributed singly along stem, never in clusters of fascicles; flowers in heads on terminal panicles; fruit an achene about 2.5 mm long, granuliferous, with 5 or 6 ribs, without a long plumose style; shurbs 30.0 to 200.0 cm tall; occurring on plains, hills, and valleys, scattered throughout the western half of Colorado, 5,000 to 10,000 ft (1524 to 3048 m).

WILD SAGEBRUSH, *Artemesia cana* Pursh   (Asteraceae)

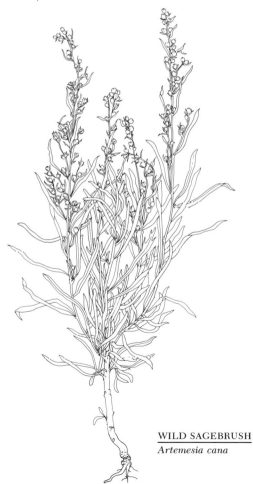

WILD SAGEBRUSH
Artemesia cana

47. Mature leaves 5.0 to 30.0 mm long, about 5 times as long as wide, margins revolute, surfaces green and shiny above, white tomentose below; leaves may be in clusters or fascicles; flowers solitary in leaf axils; fruit an achene, 6.0 to 10.0 mm long, villous, with a long plumose style 48

48. Shrubs large, to 8.0 m tall; styles on mature fruit 4.0 to 7.0 cm long; leaves 5.0 to 10.0 mm wide, oblong to lanceolate, margins slightly revolute; achenes 8.0 to 10.0 mm long at maturity; species occurring especially in the north-western quarter of Colorado, 6,500 to 9,000 ft (1981 to 2743 m).

WESTERN MOUNTAIN MAHOGANY, *Cercocarpus ledifolius* Nutt. ex T. & G.   (Rosaceae)

WESTERN MOUNTAIN MAHOGANY
Cercocarpus ledifolius

48.   Shrubs low, to 1.5 m tall; styles on mature fruit 2.0 to 4.0 cm long; leaves less than 3.0 mm wide, linear, margins distinctly revolute; achenes 6.0 to 7.0 mm long at maturity; species occurring in the far western part of Colorado, 4,500 to 8,500 ft (1372 to 2591 m).

WESTERN MOUNTAIN MAHOGANY, *Cercocarpus intricatus*
S. Wats.   (Rosaceae)

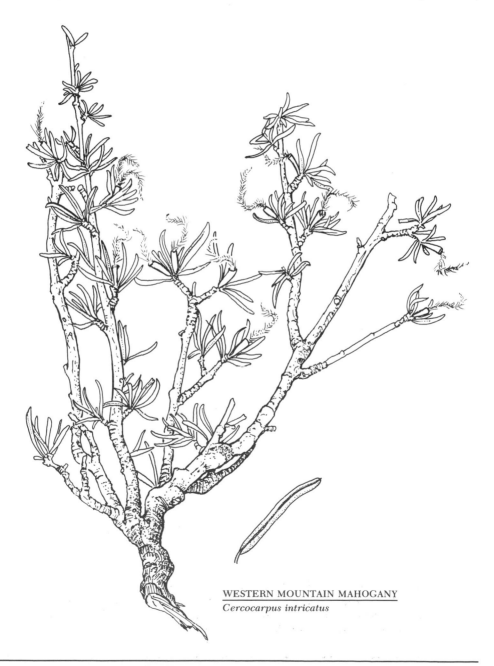

WESTERN MOUNTAIN MAHOGANY
Cercocarpus intricatus

49.   Involucral bracts 4, leaf-like, in one row; heads with 4 usually perfect flowers; leaves often in cluster of fascicles, 6.0 to 30.0 mm long; achenes silky hairy; occurring in dry ridges and plains, in western Colorado, 4,500 to 9,000 ft (1372 to 2743 m).

HORSEBRUSH, *Tetradymia canescens* DC.   (Asteraceae)

HORSEBRUSH
Tetradymia canescens

49.   Involucral bracts more than 4, in several imbricate rows [except for *Macronema discoideum* Nutt. (*Haplopappus macronema* A. Gray) with glandular, scabrous non-leaf-like involucral bracts]; heads usually with 5 or more flowers; leaves not in clusters or fascicles, variable in length 50

50.   Heads in branching, leafy panicles 8.0 to 16.0 cm long, 5.0 to 8.0 cm wide, distributed along the stems; disk flowers dioecious, white, stamens and styles extending beyond corolla so that flowers gone to seed look like yellow cotton balls; staminate involucres 3.5 mm wide; pistillate involucres 3.0 mm wide; stems striated, scurfy, often sticky with resin, eventually woody thoughout; leaf margins often with 2 to 3 coarse teeth; base of some leaf blades often tapering to a petiole 1.0 to 2.0 mm long; leaf surfaces glabrous or with scurfy scales; shrubs dense, willow-like, to 1.5 m tall, occurring in moist, saline soil, in open areas near water and in sandy soil of pastures, especially in southern half of Colorado, 3,500 to 5,500 ft (1067 to 1676 m). (See illustration, page 81.)

GROUNDSEL TREE, *Baccharis salicina* T. & G.   (Asteraceae)

50.   Heads solitary or in cymes or racemes, dense at the tips of the stems; flowers perfect, yellow; stems not striated, sometimes with ridges just below the leaf scars [except for *Xanthocephalum sarothrae* (Pursh) Shinners, a low plant from a woody caudex, which is striated and scurfy]; leaf margins never toothed; base of leaf blades clasping the stems 51

51.   Single mature head more than 1.0 cm in width at widest point, campanulate or hemispheric; heads 2 to 3 per stem or solitary on a scape 52

51.   Single mature head less than 1.0 cm in width at widest point, narrowly cylindric or tubular; heads in cymes or racemes with 4 or more heads per cluster 56

52.   Plants less than 15.0 cm tall, sometimes forming mats, not bushy in appearance; leaves mostly basal arising from a woody caudex; heads on a scape, with or without occasional leaves 53

52.   Plants more than 15.0 cm tall, usually bushy in appearance, not forming mats; leaves distributed along upright woody stems; heads 2 or 3 on a leafy stem 54

53.   Leaves glandular dotted, averaging less than 4.0 mm in width; involucral bracts 4.0 to 6.0 mm long, in 2 or 3 indefinite series, villous; achenes 2.0 to 3.5 mm long, pubescent; shrubs herbaceous above soil line, from a woody caudex, to 25.0 cm tall; occurring on sandy plains, east of Colorado Springs, 3,500 to 5,000 ft (1067 to 1524 m).

BITTERWEED, *Hymenoxys scaposa* (DC.) Parker   (Asteraceae)

53.   Leaves glabrous, not glandular dotted, averaging more than 4.0 mm in width; involucral bracts 10.0 to 11.0 mm long, in 3 or 4 definite series, leathery; achenes 4.0 to 5.0 mm long, densely silky villous; low shrubs 5.0 to 15.0 cm tall; occurring on dry hills and slopes, west of Colorado Springs, 5,000 to 8,000 ft (1524 to 2438 m).

GOLDENWEED, *Stenotus ameriodes* Nutt. [previously: *Haplopappus ameriodes* (Nutt.) A. Gray]   (Asteraceae)

BITTERWEED
Hymenoxys scaposa

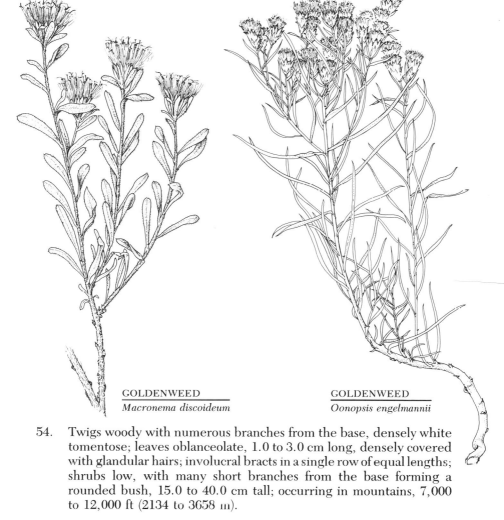

GOLDENWEED
Macronema discoideum

GOLDENWEED
Oonopsis engelmannii

54. Twigs woody with numerous branches from the base, densely white tomentose; leaves oblanceolate, 1.0 to 3.0 cm long, densely covered with glandular hairs; involucral bracts in a single row of equal lengths; shrubs low, with many short branches from the base forming a rounded bush, 15.0 to 40.0 cm tall; occurring in mountains, 7,000 to 12,000 ft (2134 to 3658 m).

GOLDENWEED, *Macronema discoideum* Nutt. (previously: *Haplopappus macronema* A. Gray)   (Asteraceae)

54. Twigs tending to be herbaceous from a woody caudex, glabrous; leaves linear or lanceolate, 3.0 to 10.0 cm long, glabrous to slightly pubescent; involucral bracts imbricate, in 3 rows and of varying length; plants, 10.0 to 30.0 cm tall; occurring in plains and hills, 4,000 to 6,000 ft (1219 to 1829 m) 55

55. Leaves linear, 1.0 to 3.0 mm wide; involucral bracts 6.0 to 8.0 mm long, 1.0 to 2.0 wide; heads at widest point 2.0 cm or less in diameter; species occurring on the plains east of Colorado Springs.

GOLDENWEED, *Oonopsis engelmannii* (A. Gray) Greene [previously: *Haplopappus engelmannii* (Gray) Hall]   (Asteraceae)

55.   Leaves lanceolate, 5.0 to 15.0 mm wide; involucral bracts 10.0 to 18.0 mm long, 3.0 to 4.0 mm wide; heads at widest point 2.5 cm or more in diameter; species occurring on plains southeast of Colorado Springs.

GOLDENWEED, *Oonopsis fremontii* (A. Gray) Greene (previously: *Haplopappus fremontii* A. Gray)   (Asteraceae)

GOLDENWEED
Oonopsis fremontii

56. Shrubs woody over the lower half of the plant or only near the base; ray flower petals or ligules inconspicuous, often lost in drying, 2.5 mm long, 1.0 mm wide; leaves scabrous, slightly barbed along the margin, rough to the touch; stems striated; a weed of the plains, overgrazed pastures and roadcuts, usually in gravel or sandy soil, 4,000 to 10,000 ft (1219 to 3048 m).

SNAKEWEED, *Xanthocephalum sarothrae* (Pursh) Shinners [previously: *Gutierrezia sarothrae* (Pursh) Britt. & Rusby]   (Asteraceae)

SNAKEWEED
Xanthocephalum sarothrae

56. Shrubs woody throughout; ray flowers absent; leaves glabrous or soft pubescent; stems not striated, sometimes with ridges just below leaf scars 57

57.   Stems tomentose or felt-like at least at nodes and axils of leaves 58

57.   Stems glabrous, glandular dotted or finely to roughly pubescent, not tomentose and felt-like 59

     58.   Heads in elongated leafy racemes at the ends of branches; outer involucral bracts commonly prolonged into slender herbaceous tips with a thin and translucent margin; flowers 5 to 20 per head; shrubs 20.0 to 60.0 cm tall; occurring on dry hills, plains to subalpine, 5,000 to 9,500 ft (1524 to 2896 m).

     RABBITBRUSH, *Chrysothamnus parryi* (A. Gray) Greene   (Asteraceae)

RABBITBRUSH
Chrysothamnus parryi

58.   Heads in round-topped cymes or corymbs at the ends of branches; involucral bracts lacking herbaceous, elongated tips; flowers 4 to 6 per heads; shrubs 20.0 to 200.0 cm tall; occurring on dry hills, plains to subalpine, 5,000 to 10,000 ft (1524 to 3048 m).

RABBITBRUSH, *Chrysothamnus nauseosus* (Pall.) Britt.   (Asteraceae)

RABBITBRUSH
Chrysothamnus nauseosus

59. Involucres 9.0 to 13.0 mm tall, bracts strongly keeled, in 5 distinct vertical rows; stems scabrous; leaves 4 or less times as long as wide, finely pubescent; low shrubs 10.0 to 30.0 cm tall; occurring in western Colorado on plains, hills, and mountains, 6,500 to 8,000 ft (1981 to 2438 m).

RABBITBRUSH, *Chrysothamnus depressus* Nutt.   (Asteraceae)

RABBITBRUSH
Chrysothamnus depressus

59. Involucres 5.0 to 9.0 mm tall, bracts moderately keeled, not in distinct vertical rows; stems glabrous to puberulent; leaves 6 or more times long as wide, scabrous-ciliate or glabrous to puberulent 60

60. Heads less than 8.0 mm long; leaves narrowly linear, flat, less than 1.0 mm wide, surface scabrous-ciliate; corollas 4.0 to 4.5 mm long; shrubs less than 35.0 cm tall; occurring on dry hills and plains in western Colorado, 5,000 to 8,500 ft (1524 to 2591 m).

RABBITBRUSH, *Chrysothamnus greenei* (A. Gray) Greene   (Asteraceae)

RABBITBRUSH
Chrysothamnus greenei

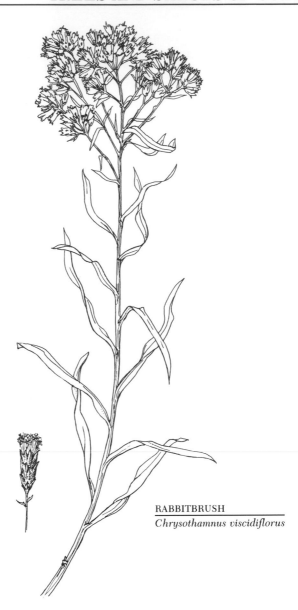

RABBITBRUSH
Chrysothamnus viscidiflorus

60.   Heads 10.0 to 15.0 mm long; leaves lanceolate, twisted, more than
      1.0 mm wide, surface glabrous to puberulent; corollas 4.5 to 7.0
      mm long; shrub from 10.0 to 240.0 cm tall; occurring on dry hills
      and plains to alkaline lowlands in western Colorado, 5,000 to 9,500
      ft (1524 to 2896 m).

      RABBITBRUSH, *Chrysothamnus viscidiflorus* (Hook.) Nutt.   (Asteraceae)

61.   Leaves with 3 to 7 nearly equal main veins from near the base 62

61.   Leaves with 1 main vein (midrib) from near the the base 65

GROUNDSEL TREE
Baccharis salicina

62. Plants shrubs to 1.5 m tall; 3 main veins, the side veins often obscure; leaf blades 3.5 to 4.0 cm long, 0.6 to 1.3 cm wide, elliptic to narrowly obovate, base tapering to the petiole, margins occasionally with 2 or 3 coarse teeth; petioles less than 2.0 mm long, sometimes obscure; fruit an achene; shrubs dense and willow-like; native to Colorado in open areas near water, occurring south of Colorado Springs, 3,500 to 5,500 ft (1067 to 1676 m).

GROUNDSEL TREE, *Baccharis salicina* T. & G.   (Asteraceae)

62. Plants trees to 8.0 m tall; 3 to 7 main veins, of which at least 3 are very obvious; leaf blades 4.0 to 14.0 cm long, 2.0 to 12.0 cm wide, elliptic or ovate to broadly ovate, base cordate to truncate or oblique; petiole longer than 3.0 mm; fruit a pod or drupe 63

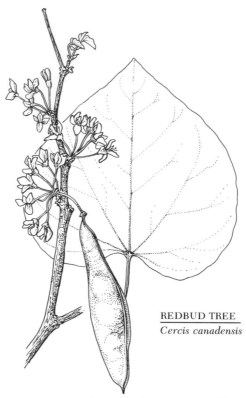

REDBUD TREE
Cercis canadensis

63.　Petiole 4.0 to 6.0 cm long; leaf base cordate, never oblique; leaf blade 8.0 to 14.0 cm long, 5.0 to 12.0 cm wide; margins of all leaves entire; bark dark gray-brown or black, smooth; flowers perfect, showy, in clusters of 4 to 8 along stems, petals purple; fruit a legume; trees to 8.0 m tall, with a broad open crown; cultivated in lawns and gardens.

REDBUD TREE, *Cercis canadensis* L.　　　　　　　　　　　(Fabaceae)

63.　Petiole less than 1.5 cm long; leaf base oblique, sometimes slightly cordate; leaf blade 4.0 to 9.0 cm long, 1.2 to 4.0 cm wide; margins of some leaves with a few teeth; bark red-brown to pale looking, ridged or striated; flowers generally monoecious with a few perfect flowers, not showy, solitary in leaf axils; petals absent 64

　　64.　Trees to 20.0 m tall with a high crown; leaf blade nearly 4 times as long as wide; leaf surface glabrous above; petioles 12.0 to 14.0 mm long; species cultivated in moist soil, on parkways and lawns.

　　　　SUGARBERRY, *Celtis laevigata* Willd.　　　　　　　　　(Ulmaceae)

　　64.　Trees 8.0 m tall with a scraggly crown; leaf blade less than 2 times as long as wide; leaf surface scabrous above; petioles 3.0 to 8.0 mm long; species native to Colorado on dry, rocky hillsides and ravine banks, occasionally in sandy soil, 4,000 to 7,200 ft (1219 to 2195 m).

　　　　NETLEAF HACKBERRY, *Celtis reticulata* Torr.　　　　　　(Ulmaceae)

<u>NETLEAF HACKBERRY</u>
Celtis reticulata

65. Buds with several overlapping scales; individual seeds not covered with long hairs; flowers perfect or imperfect, solitary, four to a cluster or in terminal panicles or spikes, but not borne in catkins; fruit a utricle, an achene, a septicidal capsule, or berry-like with seed-like nutlets; plants monoecious, dioecious, or with perfect flowers, usually shrubs 66

65. Buds enclosed by a single hoodlike scale; individual seeds covered with long hairs; flowers unisexual, borne in catkins, lacking a perianth; fruit a capsule which is not septicidal; plants dioecious trees or shrubs. This statement describes the willows (genus *Salix* L.). Pistillate catkins are needed to identify most species 70

66. Leaf blades less than 6.0 mm wide, linear to narrowly oblanceolate, resinous, aromatic; leaf margins revolute; leaf surfaces green and shiny above, densely white tomentose below; fruit a villous achene with a long plumose style; shrubs occurring in northwestern Colorado .. 67

66. Leaf blades more than 5.0 mm wide, ovate to obovate, not resinous nor aromatic; leaf margins flat; leaf surfaces glabrous or entire plant densely scurfy or mealy; fruit various, never an achene 68

67. Shrubs large, to 8.0 m tall; leaves 3.0 to 6.0 mm wide, oblong-lanceolate; leaf margins slightly revolute; styles on mature fruit 4.0 to 7.0 cm long; achene 8.0 to 10.0 mm long at maturity; species occurring in the northwestern quarter of Colorado, 6,500 to 9,000 ft (1981 to 2743 m). (See illustration, page 68.)

WESTERN MOUNTAIN MAHOGANY, *Cercocarpus ledifolius*
Nutt. ex T. & G. (Rosaceae)

67. Shrubs low, to 1.5 m tall; leaves less than 3.0 mm wide, linear; leaf margins distinctly revolute, little of the underside exposed; styles on mature fruit 2.0 to 4.0 cm long; achene 6.0 to 7.0 mm long at maturity; species occurring in the far western part of Colorado, 4,500 to 8,500 ft (1372 to 2591 m). (See illustration, page 69.)

WESTERN MOUNTAIN MAHOGANY, *Cercocarpus intricatus*
S. Wats. (Rosaceae)

68. Stems and branches white or gray, scurfy; plants woody at the base, stems tending to be herbaceous; leaves white or gray, scurfy; flowers clustered in long and narrow terminal spikes or panicles; corolla absent; fruit a utricle; shrubs to 1.0 m tall, rigid, densely branched; occurring in dry soil, in grassy barren flatlands, 4,500 to 6,000 ft (1372 to 1829 m).

SALTBUSH, *Atriplex gardneri* (Moquin) Standley (Chenopodiaceae)

68. Stems and branches red-tinged to brown, not scurfy; plants woody throughout; leaves glabrous or with a few long brown hairs; flowers solitary, in pairs, or short terminal racemes; corolla rotate or urn-shaped; fruit a capsule or an aggregate of nutlets; shrubs occurring in mountainous woods, 6,000 to 11,000 ft (1829 to 3353 m) 69

69. Shrubs with erect branches, up to 2.0 m tall; bark not separating and shredding into long thin strips; leaves thin, more than 1.0 cm wide, covered with long stiff brown hairs above; flowers solitary, in pairs from lateral buds, or several together in short terminal umbels; corolla rotate, 10.0 to 15.0 mm long; fruit a septicidal capsule; species occurring in moist woods, in the northwestern quarter of Colorado, 9,000 to 11,000 ft (2743 to 3353 m).

RHODODENDRON, *Rhododendron albiflorum* Hook.   (Ericaceae)

69. Shrubs with prostrate branches, rooting at the nodes and forming dense mats; bark on older twigs separating or shredding into long thin strips; leaves thick and leathery, less than 1.0 cm wide, glabrous on both surfaces; flowers 3 to 6 in short terminal racemes; corolla urn-shaped, 6.0 to 7.0 mm long; fruit an aggregate of nutlets; species occurring on open hillsides and woods, in semi-dry areas throughout Colorado, 6,000 to 10,000 ft (1829 to 3048 m).

KINNIKINICK, *Arctostaphylos uva-ursi* (L.) Spreng.   (Ericaceae)

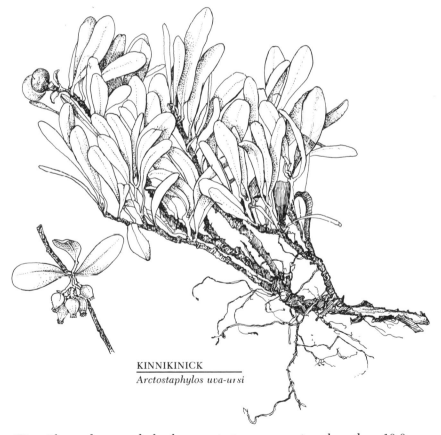

KINNIKINICK
Arctostaphylos uva-ursi

70. Plants depressed shrubs, prostrate, or creeping, less than 10.0 cm tall; alpine and subalpine species 71

70. Plants trees or shrubs, more than 10.0 cm tall; species not confined to higher elevations 72

71. Scales of the catkins pilose, brown to black; leaves slightly glaucous beneath; catkins 2.0 to 4.0 cm long, usually more than 10 flowers; styles 0.5 to 1.0 mm long; leaf apex tending toward acute; alpine plants with long, heavy, woody horizontal stems, 11,000 to 13,000 ft (3353 to 3962 m).

ARCTIC WILLOW, *Salix arctica* Pallas   (Salicaceae)

71. Scales of the catkins glabrous or nearly so, green; leaves glaucous and reticulate beneath; catkins 1.0 to 2.0 cm long, usually fewer than 10 flowers; styles lacking; leaf apex tending toward obtuse; alpine plants with short stems and with leaves clustered at the ends of creeping, slender branches, 10,500 to 12,500 ft (3200 to 3810 m).

SNOW WILLOW, *Salix reticulata* L.   (Salicaceae)

72. Older twigs pruinose, with a powdery blue-white to white covering or glaucous bloom (may be removed by rubbing the stem) 73

72. Older twigs not pruinose, lacking a glaucous bloom 75

73. Capsules on pistillate plants glabrous; mature leaves long and narrow, oblong-elliptic, tending toward linear, averaging more than 6.0 cm long; staminate catkins 1.0 to 2.0 cm long and sessile; shrubs, usually 2.0 to 4.0 m tall; common in the canyons and foothills of the front range, 5,500 to 8,500 ft (1676 to 2591 m).

BLUESTEM WILLOW, *Salix irrorata* Anderss.   (Salicaceae)

73. Capsules on pistillate plants pubescent; mature leaves short, tending toward lanceolate, averaging 4.5 cm or less long; shrubs usually 0.5 to 4.0 m tall 74

74. Mature leaves all entire, averaging 2.0 to 4.0 cm long; pistillate catkins subglobose; capsule beak averaging 10.0 to 15.0 mm long, on leafy peduncles; styles less than 0.5 mm long; staminate catkins rarely over 1.0 cm long; plants common near bogs and meadows in the front range, 6,500 to 11,000 ft (1981 to 3353 m).

GEYER WILLOW, *Salix geyeriana* Anderss.   .   (Salicaceae)

74. Mature leaves both entire and dentate-crenate, averaging 4.0 to 6.5 cm long; dark green above and glaucous to silvery pubescent below; pistillate catkins long and dense; capsule beak averaging 20.0 mm or more long, usually sessile; styles 1.0 to 1.5 mm long; staminate catkins 1.0 to 3.0 cm long; plants common near bogs and meadows in the front range, 7,500 to 11,000 ft (2286 to 3353 m).

BLUE WILLOW, SILVER WILLOW, *Salix subcoerulea* Piper
(Salicaceae)

75. Capsules pubescent 76

75. Capsules glabrous, if minutely pubescent then leaves linear to linear-lanceolate 82

SNOW WILLOW
Salix reticulata

GEYER WILLOW
Salix geyeriana

ARCTIC WILLOW
Salix arctica

77.   Leaf margins revolute; leaves linear-oblong or oblanceolate, 4.0 to 12.0
      cm long, 0.7 to 2.5 cm wide, lower surface densely white tomentose;
      twigs pubescent; anthers red or purple at maturity; pistillate catkins
      emerging with the leaves, 1.5 to 4.5 cm long; species occurring in cold
      bogs and marshy areas; our only records from South Park near Antero
      Reservoir.

HOARY WILLOW, *Salix candida* Fluegge   (Salicaceae)

HOARY WILLOW
Salix candida

77.   Leaf margins flat, not revolute, leaves broader, oblong, lanceolate, oblan-
      ceolate, elliptic, or oval, 2.0 to 8.0 cm long, 0.6 to 2.5 cm wide, lower
      leaf surface may be pubescent, but not densely white tomentose; twigs
      pubescent; anthers yellow or red at maturity; pistillate catkins 0.5 to 5.0
      cm long; species occurring above 7,000 ft (2134 to 3658 m) 78

78. Wood dark reddish-brown, bright and shiny at maturity; pistillate catkins sessile or on a short stalk, not on leafy twigs, pubescent, 2.0 to 5.0 cm long; plants often over 1.5 m high; leaves bright green and lustrous above; occurring in subalpine bogs and along streams, 7,000 to 12,000 ft (2134 to 3658 m).

  PLANE-LEAF WILLOW, *Salix planifolia* Pursh   (Salicaceae)
  [Included here is *Salix phylicifolia* ssp. *planifolia* (Pursh) Hiitonen]

78. Wood gray to light brown, glaucous to dull, but never bright and shiny; pistillate catkins on leafy young twigs, seldom sessile, pubescent, 1.0 to 4.5 cm long; plants usually less than 1.5 cm high; leaves grayish-green to green, glabrate to pubescent but not lustrous above 79

79. Petioles 5.0 to 15.0 mm long, usually yellowish; leaves dark green and glabrate above, grayish green and long pilose pubescent below, apices acute; pedicels 0.5 to 1.0 mm long; common subalpine shrub, occurring in boggy meadows, 10,000 to 11,000 ft (3048 to 3566 m).

GRAY-LEAF WILLOW, *Salix glauca* L.   (Salicaceae)

79. Petioles 1.0 to 3.0 mm long, reddish; leaves usually gray pubescent with twisted hairs on both surfaces, apices abruptly acute or obtuse; pedicels less than 0.25 mm long or absent; subalpine to alpine shrub, occurring in moist meadows or along streams, 7,500 to 12,000 ft (2286 to 3658 m).

GRAY-LEAF WILLOW *Salix brachycarpa* Nutt.   (Salicaceae)

(*Salix brachycarpa* Nutt. and *Salix glauca* L. may be a single species with elevation and habitat separating the two species.)

80. Pistillate catkins borne on short leafy peduncles, 3.0 to 8.0 cm long; leaves obovate, oblanceolate or oval, 3.0 to 7.0 cm long and 1.5 to 3.5 cm wide, dark green and glabrous above, glaucous or slightly pubescent below, becoming leathery; shrubs 3.0 to 4.0 m tall; widely distributed, occurring along streams and on drier hillsides away from streams, 6,200 to 11,000 ft (1890 to 3353 m).

  SCOULER WILLOW, *Salix scouleriana* Barratt   (Salicaceae)

80. Pistillate catkins sessile or subsessile, not borne on leafy peduncles .. 81

81. Leaves narrowly lanceolate, elliptic, or oblanceolate, 0.8 to 2.0 cm wide, dark green and glabrous above, glaucous below, apices acuminate; pistillate catkins dense; capsules 3.0 to 8.0 mm long; shrubs 2.0 to 4.0 m tall; occurring along streambanks, or in wet meadows, rare in the Front Range, 7,000 to 8,000 ft (2134 to 2438 m).

SLENDER WILLOW, MEADOW WILLOW, *Salix petiolaris*
J. E. Smith   (Salicaceae)

81.   Leaves ovate, elliptic, or narrowly obovate, 1.5 to 4.0 cm wide, dark green and lightly villous above, paler and sparsely villous below, slightly leathery, apices short acuminate or acute; pistillate catkins loose; capsules 6.0 to 10.0 mm long; on long pedicles 2.0 to 4.0 mm long; shrubs 2.0 to 3.0 m tall, with a single trunk and bushy top; occurring in wet to moist areas, along streambanks or on moist hillsides, 5,000 to 9,000 ft (1524 to 2743 m).

LONG-BEAKED WILLOW, BEBB WILLOW, *Salix bebbiana*
Sargent   (Salicaceae)

BEBB WILLOW,
LONG-BEAKED WILLOW
Salix bebbiana

GRAY-LEAF WILLOW
Salix brachycarpa

82.   Leaves linear to lanceolate, 4.0 to 13.0 cm long, many times longer than wide, margins widey dentate, remotely denticulate, or entire; capsules glabrous to slightly pubescent; styles absent; colonial or clumped shrubs; occurring in rocky or sandy soils on sandbars of rivers, along streambanks, or in ditches of the plains and foothills, 4,500 to 7,500 ft (1372 to 2286 m).

SANDBAR WILLOW, *Salix exigua* Nutt.   (Salicaceae)

A similar species, *Salix interior* Rowlee, will also key out here. These two species closely resemble each other and are often confused. It is the opinion of the author that these two species are a single species; however, further investigation is needed.

SANDBAR WILLOW
Salix exigua

82.   Leaves broader, oblong, ovate, oblanceolate, lanceolate, or elliptic; margins variable; capsules glabrous; styles present 83

83.   Leaves lanceolate, elliptic, or ovate, 2.0 to 5.0 cm long; bases acute, obtuse or slightly rounded; margins of mature leaves entire, slightly subentire to glandular; shrubs usually less than 2.0 m tall 84

83.   Leaves lanceolate, elliptic, to oblanceolate, 5.0 to 10.0 cm long; bases rounded or subcordate; margins of mature leaves entire, serrulate, or serrate; shrubs or small trees usually more than 2.0 m tall 85

WOLF'S WILLOW
Salix wolfii

84. Pistillate catkins 1.0 to 2.0 cm long; mature leaves oblanceolate, elliptical, or rarely obovate, 2.0 to 3.5 cm long, 0.5 to 1.5 cm wide; shrubs less than 1.0 m tall; occurring in boggy meadows and on slopes, particularly where snow remains late in the season, 7,000 to 11,000 ft (2130 to 3350 m).

WOLF'S WILLOW, *Salix wolfii* Bebb   (Salicaceae)

84. Pistillate catkins 2.5 to 7.0 cm long; mature leaves elliptic, narrowly ovate to broadly ovate, 3.0 to 6.0 cm long; 1.5 to 3.0 cm wide; shrubs 0.5 to 2.0 m tall; collected at only one location below Horseshoe Cirque on tundra among limestone outcrops in Park County.

YUKON WILLOW, *Salix lanata* L.   (Salicaceae)

85. Twigs, bud scales, and petioles yellowish to light brown (sometimes reddish on the sunny side), glabrous; leaves oblanceolate, lanceolate or ovate-lanceolate; capsules ovoid-conic on pedicels 1.0 to 2.5 mm long; shrubs or small trees 3.0 to 5.0 m tall; occurring in the foothills and mountains, 7,000 to 8,000 ft (2134 to 2438 m).

YELLOW WILLOW, *Salix lutea* Nutt.   (Salicaceae)

YUKON WILLOW
Salix lanata

85.   Twigs reddish-brown to dark brown, glabrous to pubescent; leaves oblong-lanceolate to strap-shaped; capsules lanceoloid on pedicels 2.0 to 4.0 mm long; shrubs 2.0 to 3.0 m tall; occurring along streambanks in canyons or plains, 5,000 to 7,500 ft (1524 to 2286 m).

TONGUE-LEAVED YELLOW WILLOW, *Salix ligulifolia* (Ball)
Ball ex E. C. Smith
(Salicaceae)

86.   Stems or branches with spines or thorns 87

86.   Stems or branches without spines or thorns 92

87.   Spines 3-parted, present at most of the nodes, slender, 3.0 to 15.0 mm
       long; leaf margins dentate to nearly entire; mature leaf blades less than
       1.5 cm wide, base tapering onto the petiole; petioles 2.0 to 3.0 mm long;
       leaves may be in cluster above the spines, fruit a few-seeded berry; shrubs
       50.0 to 200.0 cm tall; native to the mountains and valleys of southwestern
       Colorado, 5,400 to 8,500 ft (1646 to 2591 m). (See illustration, page 61.)

       BARBERRY, *Berberis fendleri* A. Gray   (Berberidaceae)

87.   Spines 1-parted, present at the internodes or at the ends of twigs, stout,
       longer than 6.0 mm; leaf margins crenate or serrate to double serrate;
       mature leaf blades more than 1.0 cm wide, base distinct from petiole;
       petioles 8.0 to 20.0 mm long; fruit a pome or a fleshy drupe; small trees
       or shrubs over 200.0 cm tall 88

    88.   Petioles with glands near the junction of the blades and the petioles;
           lenticels large, prominent, horizontal; leaf blades elliptic; stipules in
           younger leaves linear, toothed, divided into 2 to 3 segments, some-
           times absent on older leaves; fruit a fleshy drupe, red to reddish-
           orange; tall shrub or tree to 5.0 m; frequently forming thickets in
           the eastern half of Colorado, 3,500 to 6,000 ft (1067 to 1829 m). (See
           illustration, page 113.)

           WILD PLUM, *Prunus americana* Marsh.   (Rosaceae)

    88.   Petioles without glands; lenticels small, light colored, neither prom-
           inent nor horizontal; leaf blades elliptic-oblanceolate or broadly ovate
           to nearly rotund; stipules absent; fruit a pome, dark red to black;
           plants native to the western half of Colorado, or cultivated as an
           ornamental shrub; 5,500 to 8,500 ft (1676 to 2591 m) 89

89.   Mature leaf blades elliptic-oblanceolate, both surfaces glabrous, bright
       green and glossy above, paler green below; leaf margins crenate-serrate,
       teeth 6 to 8 per cm, not tipped with glands; flowers small, white, in a
       cyme; fruit a pome, bright scarlet; shrub cultivated in lawns and gardens.

       FIRE-THORN, *Cotoneaster pyracantha* (L.) Spach   (Rosaceae)

89.   Mature leaf blades broadly ovate to nearly rotund, usually with at least
       one surface tomentose or with appressed hairs, yellowish-green above,
       paler below; leaf margins sharply serrate to doubly-serrate, teeth 10 to
       11 per cm, sometimes tipped with small red glands; plants native to
       Colorado, scattered throughout western half of the state, or cultivated,
       5,000 to 8,000 ft (1524 to 2438 m) 90

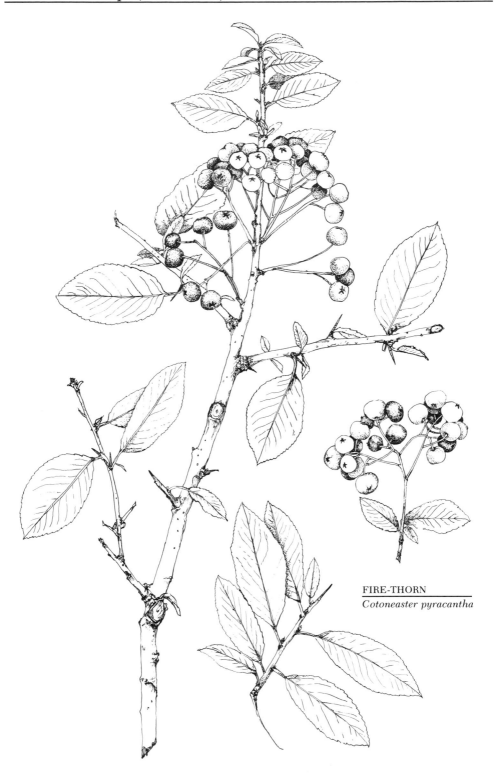

FIRE-THORN
Cotoneaster pyracantha

90. Margins once serrate, not incised with small lobes; leaves about twice as long as wide, elliptic to lanceolate; spines few, usually less than 3.0 cm long; fruit with 5 nutlets; pedicels glabrous.

HAWTHORN, RED HAW, *Crataegus rivularis* Nutt.   (Rosaceae)

90. Margins doubly serrate or incised with small lobes; leaves less than twice as long as wide, ovate to rhombic-ovate; spines many, usually more than 3.0 cm long 91

91. Surface of blade glabrous below, glabrous or with a few appressed hairs above; spines averaging less than 3.5 cm long; tips of teeth not glandular; corymb branches and pedicels glabrous while flowering; fruit with 5 nutlets, pedicels of fruit usually glabrous; species occurring on stream banks and in valleys, 5,500 to 8,000 ft (1676 to 2438 m).

RED HAW, *Crataegus erythropoda* Ashe.   (Rosaceae)

RED HAW
Crataegus erythropoda

91. Surface of blade pubescent below, especially around the veins, glabrous above; spines averaging more than 3.5 cm long; tips of teeth may be glandular; corymb branches and pedicels somewhat pubescent while flowering; fruit with 2 to 4 nutlets, pedicels of fruit often villous; species occurring on hillsides, canyons, and slopes, 5,000 to 7,000 ft (1524 to 2134 m).

WESTERN HAW, *Crataegus macracantha* Lodd.   (Rosaceae)

92.   Stems 3.0 to 30.0 cm tall; procumbent and sometimes herbaceous and matted undershrubs or small erect herbaceous shrubs; plants occurring in the high mountains, 8,000 to 14,000 ft (2438 to 4267 m) 93

92.   Stems more than 30.0 cm tall, large shrubs or trees; plants rarely occurring in the high mountains above 8,000 ft (2438 m) [except for *Betula glandulosa* Michx., a subalpine plant occurring at 7,500 to 11,000 ft (2286 to 3353 m)] 97

93.   Stems spreading, prostrate, and matted, seldom erect, undershrubs usually less than 15.0 cm tall; leaf margins coarsely crenate, or minutely crenulate to nearly entire; flowers solitary, axillary, or on naked peduncles; fruit a capsule becoming berry-like, or an achene; twigs not strongly grooved below the leaf scars 94

93.   Stems freely branching, erect, shrubs usually 15.0 to 30.0 cm tall; leaf margins finely serrulate; flowers solitary, axillary; fruit a berry with 10 to 20 seeds; twigs strongly grooved below the leaf scars 95

94.   Leaf blades orbicular to oval, glossy and leathery on both surfaces, veins inconspicuous; leaf margins crenulate or serrulate to nearly entire, flat; leaves with wintergreen flavor; petioles less than 2.0 mm long, sometimes indistinct; fruit berry-like, red; uncommon species, 10,000 to 11,500 ft (3048 to 3505 m).

CREEPING WINTERGREEN, *Gaultheria humifusa*
(R. Graham) Rydb.   (Ericaceae)

MOUNTAIN AVENS
Dryas octopetala

CREEPING WINTERGREEN
Gaultheria humifusa

94.   Leaf blades oblong to elliptic-oblong, dull and glabrous above, white-tomentose below, veins conspicuous; leaf margins coarsely crenate, somewhat revolute; petioles 8.0 to 15.0 mm long; fruit a 1-seeded achene, not red; common species on the tundra, 11,500 to 14,000 ft (3505 to 4267 m).

         MOUNTAIN AVENS, *Dryas octopetala* L.   (Rosaceae)

95.   Fruit dark blue to purple at maturity, with a bloom; branches round in cross-section; occurring in the mountains above 8,000 ft (2438 m).

     GROUSEBERRY, HUCKLEBERRY, *Vaccinium cespitosum* Michx.

                                                  (Ericaceae)

95.   Fruit red or black at maturity, glossy, without a bloom; branches strongly angled longitudinally in cross-section 96

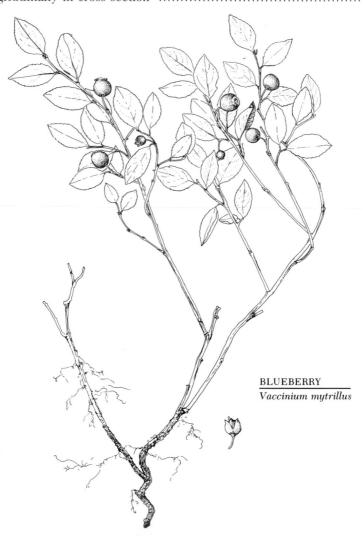

BLUEBERRY
Vaccinium mytrillus

96.   Fruit black; branches less numerous, thicker, less sharply angled; grooves of branches usually puberulent; leaves usually more than 12.0 mm long; plants scattered throughout Colorado; 8,000 to 12,000 ft (2438 to 3658 m).

BLUEBERRY, *Vaccinium myrtillus* L.   (Ericaceae)

96.   Fruit red; branches numerous, slender, sharply angled; grooves of branches usually glabrous; leaves usually less than 12.0 mm long; plants found especially in the northwestern quarter of Colorado.

WHORTLEBERRY, *Vaccinium scoparium* Leiberg   (Ericaceae)

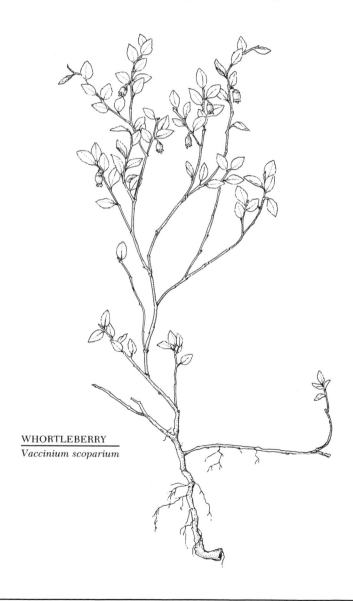

WHORTLEBERRY
Vaccinium scoparium

97.   Leaves with 3 to 7 main veins from near the base 98

97.   Leaves with 1 main vein (midrib) from near the base 107

     98.   Plants less than 2.5 m tall, shrubs, some tending to be herbaceous, but always woody at base 99

     98.   Plants more than 2.5 m tall, trees, woody throughout 102

99.   Leaf base acute to rounded; inflorescence a corymb or panicle; fruit a dry capsule; older wood dark brown to dark gray 100

99.   Leaf base cordate, hastate to truncate; inflorescence a head of 10 to 40; fruit an achene; mature wood tan to light gray 101

     100.   Leaf blades 1.0 to 2.0 cm wide, upper surface not glossy, usually pubescent; leaf margins serrate, teeth 7 to 10 per cm, callous tipped; petioles 3.0 to 5.0 mm long; buds woolly, red-brown beneath the hairs; shrubs to 70 cm tall; occurring on plains and hills, often in sandy soil, 5,000 to 7,500 ft (1524 to 2286 m).

NEW JERSEY TEA, *Ceanothus herbaceus* Raf.   (Rhamnaceae)

NEW JERSEY TEA
Ceanothus herbaceus

100. Leaf blades 3.0 to 4.5 cm wide, upper surface glossy and glabrous; leaf margins serrate, teeth 10 to 13 per cm, gland tipped; petioles 10.0 to 14.0 mm long; buds naked, bud scales in a series of small bract-like leaves; shrubs 1.0 to 3.0 m tall, basal branches low and sometimes prostrate; occurring on hillsides and mountain slopes, 6,500 to 9,000 ft (1981 to 2743 m).

GREASEWOOD, STICKY LAUREL, *Ceanothus velutinus* Dougl.
(Rhamnaceae)

GREASEWOOD, STICKY LAUREL
Ceanothus velutinus

101. Leaves lanceolate, base truncate, sub-cordate to slightly hastate, tending to extended acute at the apex; heads 1.0 cm or more in length, with more than 20 flowers per head and tending to nod; occurring in canyons on rocky slopes, 5,000 to 10,000 ft (1525 to 3048 m).

BRICKELLIBUSH, *Brickellia grandiflora* (Hook.) Nutt.   (Asteraceae)

101. Leaves deltoid-ovate, cordate to truncate at base, rounded at the apex; heads 0.7 cm or less in length, with less than 20 flowers per head and in short upright clusters; occurring on dry slopes, on rocky mesas in the foothills; western and southern part of Colorado, 5,500 to 7,000 ft (1675 to 2135 m).

BRICKELLIBRUSH, *Brickellia californica* (T. & G.) Gray   (Asteraceae)

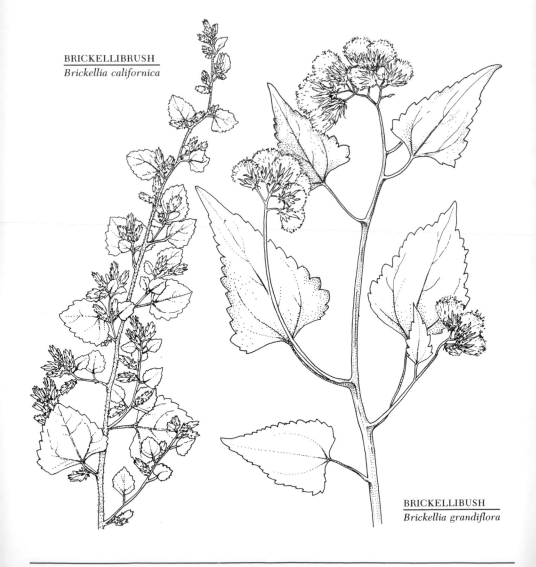

BRICKELLIBRUSH
Brickellia californica

BRICKELLIBUSH
Brickellia grandiflora

102. Petioles usually flattened; leaf base deltoid; leaves wider than long; fruit a catkin 103

102. Petioles not flattened; leaf base oblique; leaves usually longer than wide; fruit a nutlet, drupe, multiple, or if a catkin then leaf base oblique 105

103. Trees occurring in the mountains, on slopes and in valleys, 6,000 to 10,000 ft (1829 to 3048 m); young bark greenish-white or cream-colored, marked with dark, raised, eye-shaped branch scars; twigs slender, reddish; leaf blades suborbicular to orbicular, base rounded; leaf surfaces bright green above, dull green below; leaf margins with shallow teeth, sometimes nearly undulate.

QUAKING ASPEN, *Populus tremuloides* Michx.   (Salicaceae)

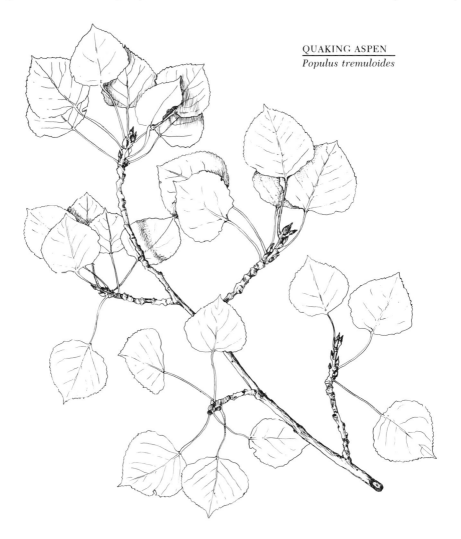

QUAKING ASPEN
Populus tremuloides

103. Trees occurring on the plains, in valleys, in riverbottoms, 3,500 to 7,000 ft (1067 to 2134 m); young bark not marked by eye-shaped protruberances; twigs stout, yellowish; leaf blades deltoid to deltoid-ovate, base truncate to cordate; leaf surfaces yellowish or light green on both sides; leaf margin toothed 104

    104. Leaves with not more than 10 teeth on each side of the blade; petioles lacking glands; pedicels shorter than the capsules; species growing on the plains and in river bottoms in eastern Colorado, 3,500 to 6,000 ft (1067 to 1829 m).

    PLAINS COTTONWOOD, *Populus sargentii* Dode   (Salicaceae)

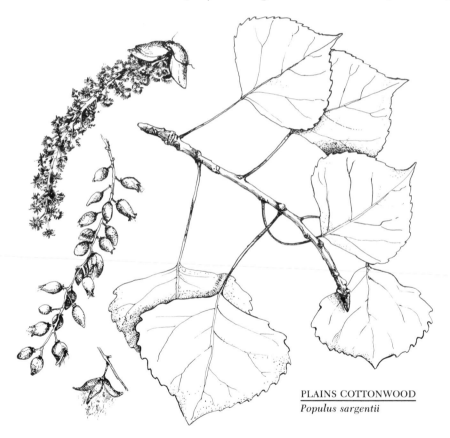

PLAINS COTTONWOOD
Populus sargentii

    104. Leaves with more than 10 teeth on each side of the blade; petioles with 2 glands usually present at the junction of the blade and petiole; pedicels equaling or longer than the capsules; species growing in valleys and on river banks in southern and western Colorado, 4,000 to 7,000 ft (1219 to 2134 m).

    SOUTHERN COTTONWOOD, *Populus deltoides* Marsh.   (Salicaceae)

    (*Populus sargentii* and *Populus deltoides* are now considered by most authorities to be a single species.)

105. Juice milky; fruit a succulent multiple, edible; leaves, at least a few, usually lobed; leaf margins serrate to crenate, leaf tip blunt or short pointed; plants monoecious or dioecious; pistillate catkins 2.5 to 4.0 cm long, axillary on new twigs, and densely flowered; species introduced from Asia in our area, cultivated in lawns and escaping to roadsides and open ground. (See illustration, page 42.)

WHITE MULBERRY, RED MULBERRY, *Morus alba* L.   (Moraceae)

105. Juice not milky; fruit a globular drupe or a nutlet suspended from a winged bract; leaves never lobed; leaf margins serrate to entire, leaf tip long tapering or abruptly tapering to a sharp point; flowers perfect, not in dense clusters 106

106. Petioles 3.0 to 7.0 cm long; veins 5 to 7, connected by parallel veins running perpendicular to main veins and forming a ladder-like pattern, vein axils with tufts of hair; leaf blades 10.0 to 14.0 cm long, 9.0 to 13.0 cm wide, tip abruptly pinched into a short sharp point; leaf margins serrate, teeth 6 to 8 per cm, often prolonged; older bark of trunk with shallow furrows and flat-topped ridges, but not high corky ridges; fruit a small nut attached to a wing-like leaf; trees to 20.0 m tall, cultivated as a shade tree.

BASSWOOD, LINDEN, *Tilia americana* L.   (Tiliaceae)

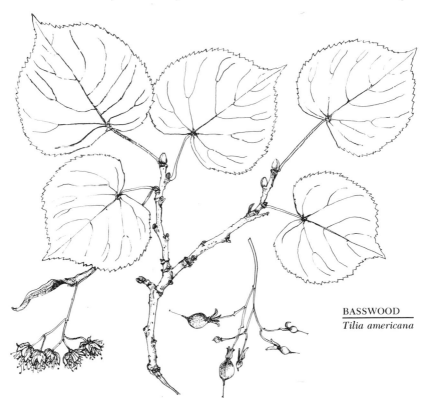

BASSWOOD
Tilia americana

106. Petioles 4.0 to 12.0 mm long; veins 3, connected by an irregular net of veins, not forming a ladder-like pattern, vein axils lacking hairs; leaf blades 5.0 to 12.0 cm long, 3.0 to 6.0 cm wide, tip tapering to a point; leaf margins dentate, teeth 2 to 4 per cm; older bark of trunk with high corky or warty ridges; fruit a drupe with thin flesh and a hard-shelled seed; trees to 25.0 m tall; native plant, scattered throughout Colorado, 4,000 to 7,200 ft (1219 to 2195 m).

HACKBERRY, *Celtis occidentalis* L.   (Ulmaceae)

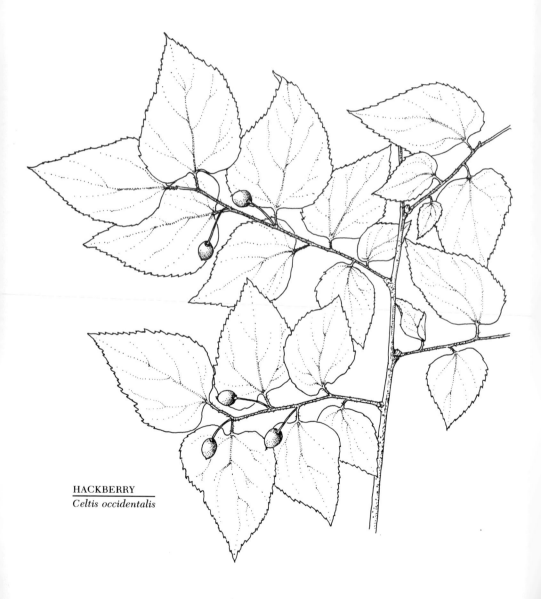

HACKBERRY
Celtis occidentalis

107. Buds with several overlapping scales; flowers perfect or imperfect, solitary, few to a cluster, in terminal panicles or spikes, or if borne in catkins then drooping with flowers on broad cup-shaped disks; floral bracts lobed or coarsely ciliate; fruit an utricle, capsule, achene, or berry-like with seed-like nutlets; plants monecious, dioecious, or with perfect flowers 108

107. Buds enclosed by a single hood-like scale; flowers unisexual, lacking a perianth, borne in erect catkins with flowers not borne on disks; floral bracts entire or merely denticulate; fruit a capsule, individual seed covered with long hairs; plants dioecious trees or shrubs. This statement describes the willows (genus *Salix* L.). Pistillate catkins are needed to identify some species 130

   108. Margins of leaves doubly serrate, doubly dentate and/or incised with reduced lobes; blades usually more than 3.5 cm wide 109

   108. Margins of leaves once serrate, crenate, or serrulate; blades usually less than 4.0 cm wide 113

109. Leaf margins doubly dentate, but not incised with small lobes; leaf bases oblique (in **CHINESE ELM** *Ulmus parvifolia* Jacq. not all leaves will show this characteristic); fruit a 1-seeded samara, with the wing surrounding the seed; plants cultivated as shade trees along streets and lawns 110

109. Leaf margin incised with small lobes, margins doubly serrate or dentate; leaf bases not oblique; fruit a nut or nutlet, may be surrounded by wings or bracts; plants native to Colorado, occurring in woods and moist areas .. 112

   110. Leaves rough and scabrous on the upper surface, 10.0 to 13.0 cm long; buds brown, rusty-pubescent or tomentose; petioles stout, 3.0 to 5.0 mm long, pubescent; trees to 20.0 m tall; occasionally introduced to our area.

      SLIPPERY ELM, RED ELM, *Ulmus rubra* Muhl.   (Ulmaceae)

   110. Leaves smooth and glabrous or nearly so on the upper surface, 4.0 to 12.0 cm long; buds glabrous to slightly pubescent; petioles 2.0 to 8.0 mm long, glabrous or pubescent 111

111. Mature leaf buds ovoid, 2.0 to 3.0 mm long, dark brown, usually ciliate; leaves 4.0 to 8.0 cm long, often not strongly oblique at the base; samara glabrous, with a slight notch but the sinus closed; small trees or shrubs to 15.0 m, commonly with many branches from the base; introduced and escaping cultivation.

SIBERIAN ELM, CHINESE ELM, *Ulmus pumila* L.   (Ulmaceae)

Another cultivated species in our area, **CHINESE ELM** *Ulmus parvifolia* Jacq., is similar to *Ulmus pumila*. However, this species is a fall flowering tree with flowers in racemes compared to *Ulmus pumila*, a spring flowering tree with flowers in clusters from the previous year's buds.

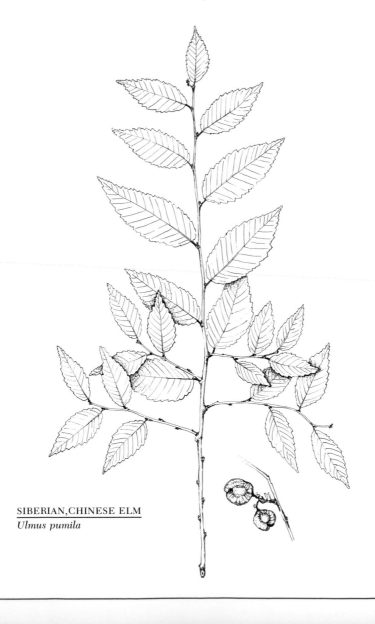

SIBERIAN, CHINESE ELM
Ulmus pumila

111. Mature leaf buds acute to elongate, 2.0 to 3.0 mm long, gray to light brown, glabrous to ciliate; leaves 7.0 to 12.0 cm long, oblique at the base; samara slightly pubescent, with a notch at the apex and the sinus usually open; large trees to 25.0 m tall, with one large trunk; cultivated in lawns and along streets.

AMERICAN ELM, *Ulmus americana* L.   (Ulmaceae)

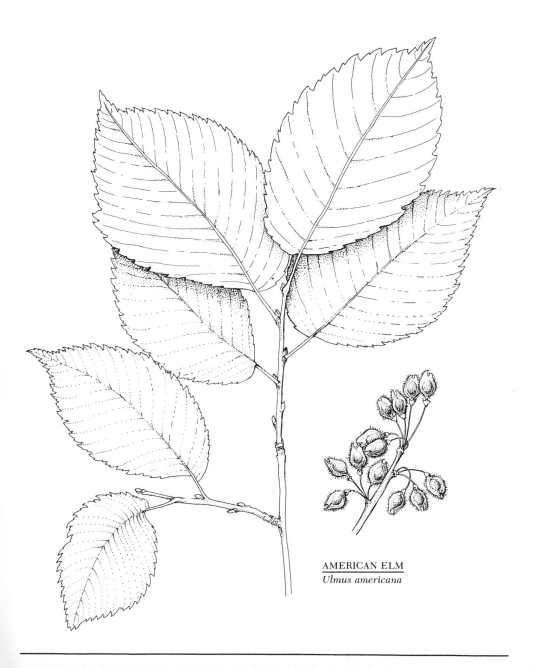

AMERICAN ELM
Ulmus americana

112. Leaf apices abruptly pinched into a point, base cordate to rounded; staminate flowers in catkins; pistillate flowers few, in scaly buds sessile on twigs; buds 3.5 to 5.0 mm long, not stalked, many scales, densely ciliate; fruit a nut, 10.0 to 15.0 mm long, enclosed by bristly, wing-like bracts; shrub to 2.5 m tall, in loose thickets; plants occurring in moist soil on creek banks and hillsides, mostly in the eastern foothills, 5,400 to 8,000 ft (1646 to 2438 m).

HAZELNUT, *Corylus cornuta* Marsh.　　　　　　(Betulaceae)

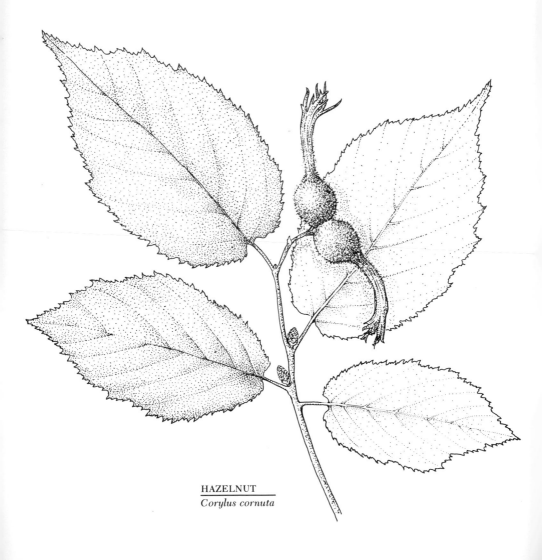

HAZELNUT
Corylus cornuta

112. Leaf apices broadly curving to a point, base broadly tapering to rounded; staminate and pistillate flowers in catkins; buds 1.0 to 12.0 mm long, stalked, two scales, valvate, sparsely pubescent or scurfy; fruit a nutlet, 14.0 to 18.0 mm long, in cone-like catkins; large shrubs or small trees to 10.0 m tall, with clustered twigs; plants occurring in swampy ground or sandy soil, mostly in the mountains, 5,000 to 10,000 ft (1524 to 3048 m).

ALDER, *Alnus tenuifolia* Nutt.   (Betulaceae)

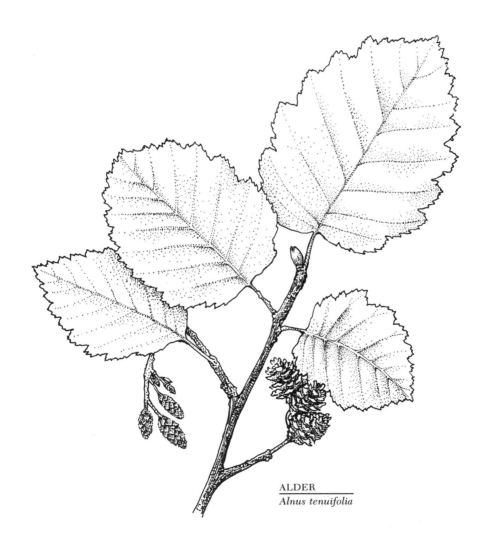

ALDER
Alnus tenuifolia

114. Flowers and fruit many, borne in racemes terminating a new leafy branch; fruit dark purple to black, glossy; flowers pubescent, petals 3.0 mm long, pedicels 5.0 mm or less long; buds conical, 4.0 to 8.0 mm long, scales light brown with greyish edges; leaf margins finely and sharply serrate or dentate, teeth 5 to 10 per cm, pointing outward or toward the apex; trees to 6.0 m tall, but often growing in thickets with the tallest tree 3.0 m tall; species occurring on roadsides or borders of woods; scattered throughout Colorado, 4,500 to 9,000 ft (1372 to 2743 m).

CHOKE CHERRY, *Prunus virginiana* L.   (Rosaceae)

114. Flowers and fruit few, borne in umbellate clusters, the clusters at the end of a spur or from lateral buds; fruit bright red to orange, or purplish-black; flowers glabrous or nearly so, petals more than 5.0 mm long, pedicels 8.0 mm or more long; buds ovoid to obovoid, 4.0 mm or less long, scales reddish to dark brown 115

115. Plants low prostrate shrubs to 1.0 m tall; mature leaf blades 3.0 to 6.0 cm long and usually 2.0 cm or less wide; leaf margins finely serrate, teeth 6 to 8 per cm, teeth longer toward leaf base; buds 1.0 to 2.0 mm long, often 2 or 3 in the leaf axils, tips rounded, margin of scales keeled; fruit a deep purple cherry without a ventral groove, 13.0 to 14.0 mm long, glossy; species occurring on sandy or gravelly prairie hillsides, often hidden in tall grasses, 3,500 to 6,500 ft (1067 to 1981 m).

DWARF CHERRY, SAND CHERRY, *Prunus besseyi* Barley   (Rosaceae)

115. Plants trees to 8.0 m tall, usually in thickets; mature leaf blades usually more than 2.0 cm wide; leaf margins doubly serrate to crenate-teeth uniform to leaf base; buds 2.5 to 5.0 mm long; fruit a purple plum more than 2.0 cm long, or a red cherry less than 8.0 mm long; species occurring in moist woods, on banks, and in valleys 116

116. Fruit a plum with a ventral groove, purple glaucous, 2.0 to 3.0 cm long; young leaves and twigs pubescent, leaf blades remaining pubescent below, especially along the midrib; twigs may have spines; buds often 2 or 3 in a leaf axil, rounded, 2.5 mm long; leaf margins sharply or doubly serrate, teeth 3 to 6 per cm, without glands; species occurring 3,500 to 6,000 ft (1067 to 1829 m).

WILD PLUM, *Prunus americana* Marsh   (Rosaceae)

116. Fruit a cherry without a ventral groove, red, glossy, 3.0 to 5.0 mm long; young leaves and twigs glabrous; twigs without spines; buds only 1 to a leaf axil, pointed, 3.0 to 5.0 mm long; leaf margins crenate-serrate, teeth 10 to 13 per cm, with large triangular glands; species occurring 5,500 to 8,500 ft (1676 to 2591 m).

PIN CHERRY, BIRD CHERRY, *Prunus pensylvanica* L.   (Rosaceae)

PIN CHERRY,
BIRD CHERRY
Prunus pensylvanica

WILD PLUM
Prunus americana

CHOKE CHERRY
Prunus virginiana

DWARF CHERRY,
SAND CHERRY
Prunus besseyi

117. Lower surface of leaves, petioles, and young shoots permanently and densely white tomentose; leaf margins crenate-serrate to the base, 6 to 8 teeth per cm; leaf blades oblong-ovate, less than twice as long as wide, base rounded to cordate; petioles deeply channeled from the base of the blade; flowers showy, petals white to pinkish, 8.0 to 12.0 mm long; fruit a fleshy pome, 3.0 cm or more in diameter, red; trees escaping cultivation to roadsides, borders of woods or clearings. The **WILD CRABAPPLE TREE** *Pyrus ioensis* (Wood) Barley, may also occur, rarely, in our area and will key out here.

APPLE, *Pyrus malus* L.　　　　　　　　　　　　　　　　(Rosaceae)

APPLE
Pyrus malus

117. Lower surface of leaves, petioles, and young shoots glabrous to slightly pubescent; leaf margins coarsely serrate only halfway to the base of the blades with 4 to 5 teeth per cm and blades less than twice as long as wide, or margins finely serrulate to the base with 6 to 20 teeth per cm and blades at least twice as long as wide; leaf base cuneate to truncate; petioles not deeply channelled from the base of the blade; fruit an achene, follicle, drupe, or pome less than 2.0 cm in diameter 118

118. Leaves at least twice as long as wide; leaf margins finely serrate to serrulate, teeth 6 to 20 per cm extending to the base of the blade [except for *Spiraea vanhhoutii* (Briot) Zab. which has only 3 to 7 coarse teeth near the apex]; lateral veinlets becoming obscure before reaching the margin, not running parallel 119

118. Leaves obviously less than twice as long as wide; leaf margins coarsely serrate, teeth 4 to 5 per cm extending halfway to the base of the blade; lateral veinlets obvious, running parallel to each other from the midrib to the margin 126

119. Leaf margins coarsely serrate, teeth near the apex; leaves may have 3 distinct main veins, midribs not obvious and not paler than the blade; leaf blades usually 2.5 cm or less long, rhombic-ovate to obovate, dark green, glossy; flowers many, 8.0 to 10.0 mm in diameter, white, in round-topped umbels at the end of short leafy branches; fruit a follicle; shrubs to 2.0 m tall, cultivated as an ornamental plant, rarely escaping.

BRIDAL WREATH, *Spiraea vanhoutii* (Briot) Zab.   (Rosaceae)

BRIDAL WREATH
Spiraea vanhoutii

119. Leaf margins finely serrate to serrulate, teeth extending to the base of the blade; leaves distinctly with only 1 main vein, midrib very obvious at least at the base and paler than the blade; leaf blades usually more than 2.5 cm long, lanceolate to ovate to elliptic, yellow-green, not glossy; flowers solitary, or 2 to 4 in leaf axils, or many in pendulous catkins; fruit a fleshy drupe or pome, or a catkin 120

120. Trees to 20.0 m tall with 1 main trunk and a high rounded or cylindrical crown; fruit a dry capsule; seeds with a ring of silky hair at the base; plants dioecious; flowers and fruits crowded in drooping catkins; petioles 1.0 to 6.0 cm long, often flattened laterally, channeled deeply above; leaf margins with rounded, incurved teeth, a small gland or callous on the incurved tip 121

120. Shrubs to 5.0 m tall, low and spreading, or bushy, or tree-like in the thickets or colonies; fruit fleshy, a pome or drupe; seeds lacking a ring of silky hairs; flowers perfect, or if unisexual then plants dioecious, solitary or clustered in umbels of 2 to 4 in the leaf axils; petioles less than 1.0 long (except for *Prunus americana* Marsh. with petioles 9.0 to 16.0 mm long), not flattened at the sides, not channeled above 123

NARROW-LEAVED COTTONWOOD
Populus angustifolia

121. Mature leaf blades 2.5 cm or less wide; lanceolate to ovate-lanceolate to elliptic, base narrowly cuneate, with a fine clear gland at the tip; leaf margins with 7 to 9 teeth per cm, not ciliate; petioles 1.0 to 1.5 m long; trees with a conical crown to 16.0 m tall, occurring along streams, margins of marshy areas, occasionally in roadside ditches, 5,000 to 8,000 ft (1524 to 2438 m).

NARROW-LEAVED COTTONWOOD, *Populus angustifolia* James
(Salicaceae)

121. Mature leaf blades 4.5 to 6.0 cm wide, ovate to broadly ovate, base broadly cuneate to sub-cordate, lacking a clear gland at the tip; leaf margins with 2 to 5 teeth per cm, ciliate; petioles 2.0 to 6.0 cm long 122

122. Leaf surface whitish below with a conspicuous network of dark veinlets, dark or bright green above; leaf blades 8.0 to 12.0 cm long, 4.5 to 6.0 cm wide, broadly cuneate to slightly rounded to the base; petiole usually abruptly broadening at the base, often twisted; terminal buds more than 15.0 mm long, very resinous-sticky, aromatic; trees with a cylindrical crown to 20.0 m tall; occurring along streams, on moist hillsides and in canyons, 6,000 to 12,000 ft (1829 to 3658 m).

BALSAM POPLAR, *Populus balsamifera* L.   (Salicaceae)

BALSAM POPLAR
Populus balsamifera

122. Leaf surface light green below with an inconspicuous network of light veinlets, dark or bright green above; leaf blade 6.0 to 9.0 cm long, 5.0 to 6.0 cm wide, rounded to subcordate at the base; petiole uniform in width to the base, not twisted; terminal bud less than 15.0 mm long, slightly resinous, not aromatic; trees with a rounded crown to 20.0 m tall; occurring on moist or dry ground along streams, on hillsides, in valleys and usually in poor soil, 4,500 to 8,500 ft (1372 to 2291 m).

SMOOTH-BARKED COTTONWOOD, *Populus acuminata* Rydb.

(Salicaceae)

Usually considered a hybrid species between *Populus angustifolia* James and either *Populus deltoides* Marsh. var. occidentalis Rydb. or *Populus deltoides* Marsh. ssp. *wislizenii* (S. Wats.) Eckenw.

SMOOTH-BARKED COTTONWOOD
Populus acuminata

123.   Leaves in clusters or fascicles at the ends of branches; mature leaf blades 2.0 to 4.0 cm long, dark green on both sides, leathery; leaf margins serrulate to entire, teeth glandular and reddish-brown; petioles usually 2.0 mm or less long; flowers 1 to 3, clustered at the ends of branches, petals pale pink; fruit a fleshy pome, 10.0 to 15.0 mm in diameter, yellowish to reddish-brown; shrubs to 2.0 m tall, with rigid branches; occurring on hills and slopes, usually in acid soil, scattered throughout the western one-third of Colorado, 5,500 to 8,000 ft (1676 to 2438 m).

SQUAW APPLE, *Peraphyllum ramosissimum* Nutt.   (Rosaceae)

123.   Leaves attached singly along the stems, not in clusters or fascicles; mature leaf blades 3.0 to 10.0 cm long, yellowish-green and paler below, not leathery; leaf margins distinctly serrate, serrulate, or crenulate, teeth not glandular, not reddish-brown; petioles usually 4.0 mm or more long; flowers 1 to 3, clustered on pedicels or in sessile umbels in leaf axils; fruit a fleshy drupe or berry 124

   124.   Leaf margins serrulate to crenulate; leaf blades sometimes appearing to be nearly opposite; fruit a berry-like drupe with 2 to 4 nutlets, about 8.0 mm in diameter, blackish; flowers unisexual, 1 to 3 clustered on individual pedicels in leaf axils, petals 4, greenish; shrubs bushy, 2.0 to 3.0 m tall; plants occurring on moist hillsides and in valleys, especially in southwestern Colorado at about 7,000 ft (2134 m).

   BUCKTHORN, *Rhamnus smithii* Greene   (Rhamnaceae)

   124.   Leaf margins sharply serrate or occasionally doubly serrate; leaf blades always distinctly alternate; fruit a drupe with one seed, 12.0 to 25.0 mm in diameter, red to black; flowers perfect, 3 or 4 clustered in sessile umbels in leaf axils, petals 5, white or sometimes pink; shrubs low, less than 1.5 m tall, or tree-like to 5.0 m tall in dense thickets; species occurring along streams and moist places, on sandy or gravelly hillsides on the plains, 3,500 to 6,000 ft (1067 to 1829 m)   125

125.   Shrubs to 1.0 m tall, low and spreading; branches glabrous; mature leaf blades 3.0 to 6.0 cm long, 1.0 to 2.0 cm wide, both surfaces glabrous; fruit a black or reddish-black cherry without a ventral groove, stone nearly round; species occurring on sandy and gravelly hills and rocky ledges on the prairie, 3,500 to 6,500 ft (1067 to 1981 m). (See illustration, page 113.)

DWARF CHERRY, SAND CHERRY, *Prunus besseyi* Bailey   (Rosaceae)

125.   Shrubs to 5.0 m tall, tree-like forming dense thickets by sprouts from the roots; branches pubescent at least when young, sometimes spiny; mature leaf blades 6.0 to 10.0 cm long, 3.0 to 5.0 cm wide, lower surface usually pubescent, especially along midrib; fruit a red or orange plum with a ventral groove, stone flat; occurring in moist soil or along stream banks or in fence rows in woodlands, 4,000 to 6,000 ft (1219 to 1829 m). (See illustration, page 113.)

WILD PLUM, *Prunus americana* Marsh.   (Rosaceae)

126. Twigs and leaves covered with clear or brown resinous glands, glabrous; flowers monoecious, bract-like, staminate flowers in drooping catkins, pistillate flowers in erect catkins; fruit a small samara-like nutlet; species occurring in marshes, moist valleys and along streams . 127

126. Twigs and leaves not covered with resinous glands, pubescent to glabrous; flower perfect, campanulate or long cylindric, solitary, or in small clusters or fascicles, or in compound terminal panicles; fruit a pome or an achene; species occurring usually in dry to well-drained rocky soil, on hills, mesas, and canyons 128

127. Shrubs low, to 2.0 m tall, prostrate at high elevations; leaf blades 1.5 to 2.0 cm long, 1.2 to 1.8 cm wide, obovate to nearly rotund; leaf margins crenate, teeth often gland-tipped; petiole 3.0 to 6.0 mm long; fruit with a narrow wing; species occurring in marshes and moist areas along streams or in valleys, 7,500 to 11,000 ft (2286 to 3353 m).

DWARF BIRCH, MARSH BIRCH, *Betula glandulosa* Michx.　(Betulaceae)

127. Shrubs large, or small trees to 12.0 m tall; leaf blades 2.0 to 4.5 cm long, 2.0 to 3.0 cm wide, broadly ovate; leaf margins serrate to doubly serrate, teeth not gland-tipped; petiole 10.0 to 15.0 mm long; fruit with a wing wider than the nutlet; species occurring along streams in moist valleys, and on hillsides, 5,000 to 9,000 ft (1524 to 2743 m).

WESTERN BIRCH, *Betula fontinalis* Sarg.　(Betulaceae)

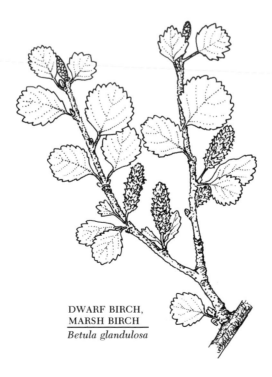

DWARF BIRCH,
MARSH BIRCH
Betula glandulosa

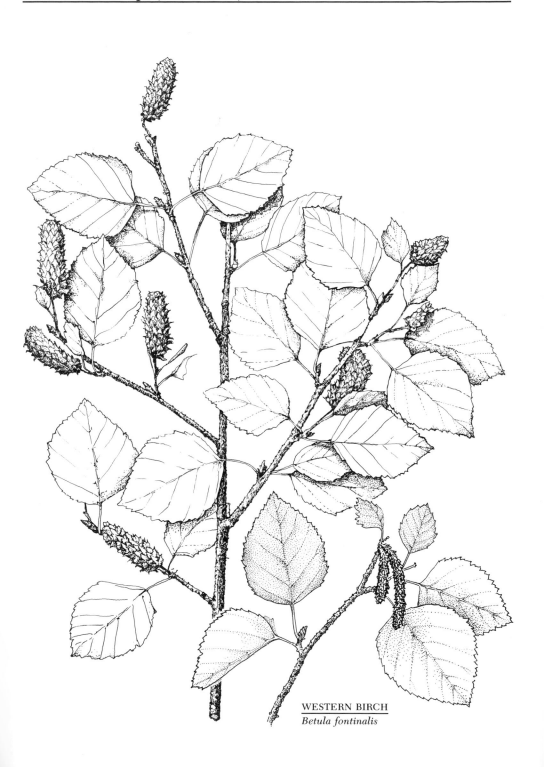

WESTERN BIRCH
Betula fontinalis

128. Leaves rounded to subcordate at the base, distinct from the petiole; leaf margins dentate to serrate; surfaces on mature leaves either both pubescent or both glabrous; petiole 8.0 to 18.0 mm long; older bark not separating and peeling into long, thin strips; flowers 2 to 10 in simple terminal racemes; fruit a pome, dark red to blackish; shrubs occurring on brushy hillsides, in open woods and along streams, 5,000 to 10,000 ft (1524 to 3048 m).

SERVICEBERRY, *Amelanchier* Medic. spp.   (Rosaceae)

The many species of *Amelanchier* are difficult to distinguish. Authorities now lump them into 3 species: *A. pumila* Nutt. ex T. & G. always has glabrous leaves and twigs; *A. utahensis* Koehne and *A. alnifolia* Nutt. which intergrade, usually have pubescent leaves and twigs.

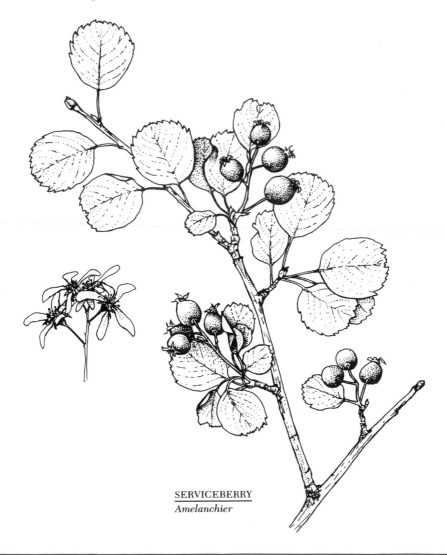

SERVICEBERRY
Amelanchier

128. Leaves distinctly cuneate at the base, decumbent on the petiole; leaf margins serrate; surfaces on mature leaves glabrous or nearly so above, closely tomentose below; petiole 3.0 to 6.0 mm long; older bark separating and peeling into long, thin strips; flowers 1 to 3 clustered in leaf axils, or many in a compound terminal panicle; fruit a villous achene 129

129. Flowers many, in a compound terminal panicle, 5.0 to 20.0 cm long, pyramid-shaped; petals white to pink; fruit an achene without a long plumose style; inflorescence and seed heads usually remaining on the plant throughout the year; mature leaves attached singly along the stems, not in cluster or fascicles; species occurring on rocky slopes throughout western Colorado, 5,500 to 10,000 ft (1676 to 3048 m).

MOUNTAIN SPRAY, *Holodiscus dumosus* (Nutt.) Heller   (Rosaceae)

MOUNTAIN SPRAY
Holodiscus dumosus

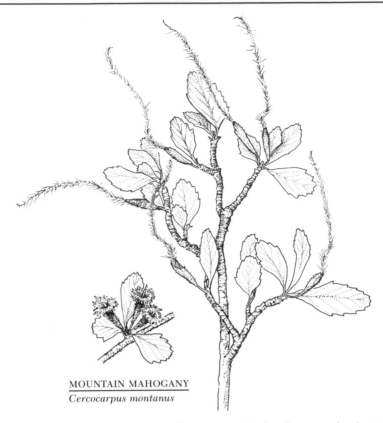

MOUNTAIN MAHOGANY
Cercocarpus montanus

129. Flowers solitary or in clusters of 2 or 3, in leaf axils on pedicels 2.0 to 5.0 mm long, pubescent; petals absent; fruit an achene with a long plumose style, usually remaining on the plant throughout the year; mature leaves often in clusters or fascicles; species occurring on eroded hillsides, open rocky woods, or stony soil thoughout Colorado, 4,000 to 8,500 ft (1219 to 2591 m).

MOUNTAIN MAHOGANY, *Cercocarpus montanus* Raf.   (Rosaceae)

130. Plants 7.0 to 15.0 m tall, trees 131

130. Plants 2.5 to 5.0, rarely 10.0, m tall, shrubs or small trees 134

131. Branches pendulous, yellowish to brownish; leaves linear-lanceolate, 0.5 to 1.5 cm wide, apices long acuminate, margins finely unevenly spinulose-serrulate; capsules 1.5 to 2.5 mm long, narrowly ovoid, sessile; styles nearly obsolete; plants introduced, cultivated in lawns.

WEEPING WILLOW, *Salix babylonica* L.   (Salicaceae)

131. Branches erect, if pendulous then only at tips, greenish, yellowish, ashy-gray, or dark red; leaves narrowly lanceolate to lanceolate or broader, 1.0 to 3.5 cm wide, apices acuminate, margins serrate to closely serrulate, not spinulose-serrulate; capsules 3.0 to 5.5 mm long, pedicellate to sub-sessile; styles 0.2 to 0.7 mm long 132

132. Petioles lacking glands near base of leaf blade, glabrous; leaf margins closely serrulate; branches somewhat drooping at ends; branchlets greenish; plants native, occurring along streams and wet places on eastern plains or in canyons of front range, 3,500 to 7,500 ft (1067 to 2286 m).

PEACH-LEAF WILLOW, *Salix amygdaloides* Anderss.   (Salicaceae)

132. Petioles with gland near base of leaf blade, pubescent to glandular; leaf margins serrate; branches always erect; plants introduced 133

133. Branchlets pubescent, greenish or yellowish; leaves serrate, 9 to 10 teeth per cm, more or less silvery-silky on both surfaces; petioles pubescent; capsules ovoid-conic, 3.5 to 5.0 mm long, nearly sessile; plants introduced, cultivated in lawns.

WHITE WILLOW, *Salix alba* var. *vitellina* (L.) Stokes   (Salicaceae)

133. Branchlets glabrous, greenish to dark red; leaves serrate, 5 to 6 teeth per cm, glabrous with some raised glands; petioles glabrous; capsules narrow conic, 4.0 to 5.5 mm long; peduncles 0.5 to 1.0 mm long; twigs brittle; plants introduced, cultivated in lawns.

CRACK WILLOW, BRITTLE WILLOW, *Salix fragilis* L.   (Salicaceae)

CRACK WILLOW,
BRITTLE WILLOW
Salix fragilis

134. Shrubs 1.0 to 2.5 m tall, with many stems; leaves sub-opposite, linear to linear-oblanceolate or spatulate, 0.4 to 1.5 mm wide, short petiolate; capsules sessile, 3.0 to 4.0 mm long; styles 0.1 to 0.2 mm long; plants introduced and cultivated in the Pikes Peak region, occasionally escaping cultivation.

BASKET WILLOW, *Salix purpurea* L.   (Salicaceae)

134. Shrubs 2.0 to 6.0, rarely 8.0, m tall, with few stems; leaves definitely alternate, never linear, 1.0 cm wide or wider; petioles 3.0 mm long or longer; capsules pedicellate, 4.0 to 7.0 mm long; styles 0.5 to 1.5 mm long; plants native; occurring in wet meadows, seepage areas or along streams 135

135. Branches yellow or yellowish-green, rarely dark reddish-brown; leaf bases cordate, sub-cordate, or rounded; leaves 8.0 to 10.0 cm long; anther sometimes red-tipped; pedicels of capsules less than 1.0 mm long, pilose at base; styles 1.0 to 1.5 mm long; occurring in boggy meadows, along streambanks, or lake shores, 7,000 to 9,000 ft (2134 to 2743 m).

ROCKY MOUNTAIN WILLOW, *Salix monticola* Bebb   (Salicaceae)

ROCKY MOUNTAIN WILLOW
Salix monticola

135. Branches reddish-brown or chestnut to dark brown; leaf bases acute to rounded; leaves 2.0 to 12.0 cm long; anthers never red-tipped; pedicels of capsules 1.0 mm long or longer, glabrous; styles 0.5 to 0.7 mm long 136

WHIPLASH WILLOW
Salix caudata

136. Leaves to 12.0 cm long, 4.0 cm wide, lanceolate or oblanceolate, apices long acuminate or caudate, margins glandular serrate; petioles 2.0 to 3.0 mm long; branches thick; capsules 5.0 to 7.0 mm long; occuring in wet meadows, along streams or lakes, 5,500 to 8,500 ft (1676 to 2591 m).

WHIPLASH WILLOW, *Salix caudata* (Nutt.) Heller   (Salicaceae)

(Included here are *Salix lucida* Mehl. and *Salix lasiandra* Benth.)

136. Leaves to 6.0 cm long, 2.0 cm wide, oval-oblong, apices acute or short acuminate, margins minutely serrulate to subentire; petioles 3.0 to 8.0 mm long; branches slender, capsules 4.0 to 5.0 mm long and stalked; catkins 2.0 to 6.0 cm long; occurring in seepage areas along streams in the montane, 5,300 to 9,500 ft (1615 to 2896 m).

BOOTH'S WILLOW, *Salix boothii* Dorn   (Salicaceae)

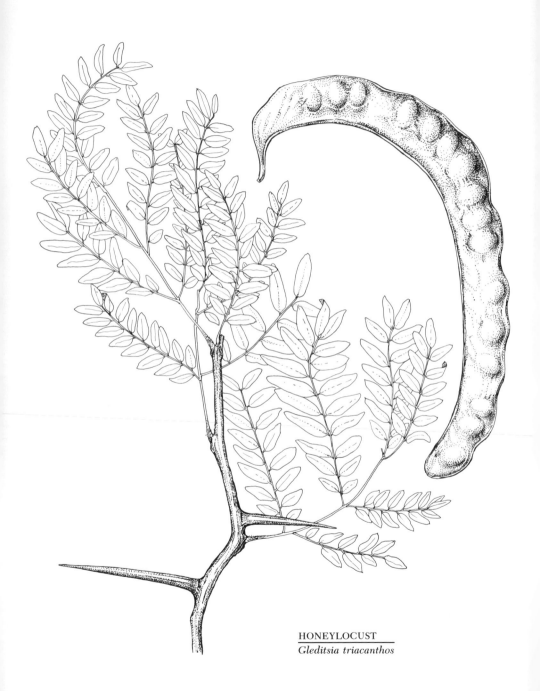

HONEYLOCUST
Gleditsia triacanthos

KEY V

Compound, Alternate, Broad Leaves

1. Leaflet margins entire 2
1. Leaflet margins serrate, dentate or undulate, never entire 10

    2. Leaves pinnately compound 3
    2. Leaves palmately compound or trifoliate 9

3. Commonly trees up to 30.0 m high; spines or thorns located on the trunk, twigs, or at the base of the leaves (cultivated species of *Robinia* L. may lack spines) 4
3. Commonly shrubs less than 3.0 m high, seldom becoming tree-like; spines or thorns lacking 6

    4. Leaves commonly even pinnate, sometimes bipinnately compound; leaflets 14 or more per leaf; fruit a curved legume, 10.0 to 40.0 cm long; often characterized by large branched spines on trunk; introduced and cultivated.

       HONEYLOCUST, *Gleditsia triacanthos* L.   (Fabaceae)

    4. Leaves commonly odd pinnate, seldom or never bipinnately compound; leaflets 19 or less per leaf; fruit a legume, less than 12.0 cm long 5

5.   Young branches, inflorescence and fruit pubescent; flowers bluish-purple; native along streams and occasionally cultivated.

       LOCUST, *Robinia neomexicana* A. Gray   (Fabaceae)

5.   Young branches, inflorescence and fruit glabrous; flowers yellow to white; cultivated near fences and buildings, escaping cultivation.

       BLACK LOCUST, *Robinia pseudoacacia* L.   (Fabaceae)

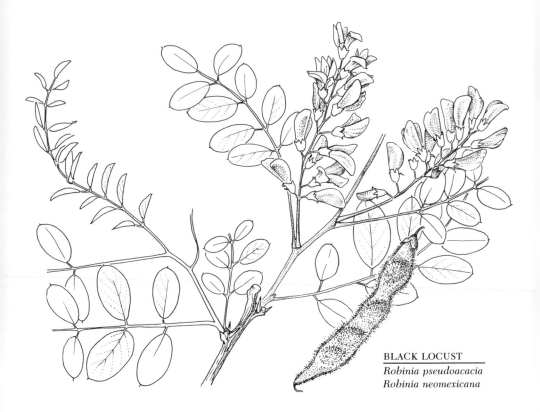

BLACK LOCUST
Robinia pseudoacacia
Robinia neomexicana

6.   Leaflets 3 to 7 per leaf, linear to lanceolate; leaves sometimes trifoliate appearing palmate; bark brown, shredding or peeling; petals 5, yellow; stamens 15 or more; fruit an achene; montane to subalpine, 7,000 to 11,500 ft (2134 to 3505 m).

       SHRUBBY CINQUEFOIL, *Pentaphylloides floribunda* (Pursh)
       A. Love   (Rosaceae)

6.   Leaflets 7 or more per leaf, oblong to oval; bark reddish-brown or brown to gray, not shredding; petals yellow, purple or purplish-blue to blue, sometimes white; stamens 10; fruit a legume 7

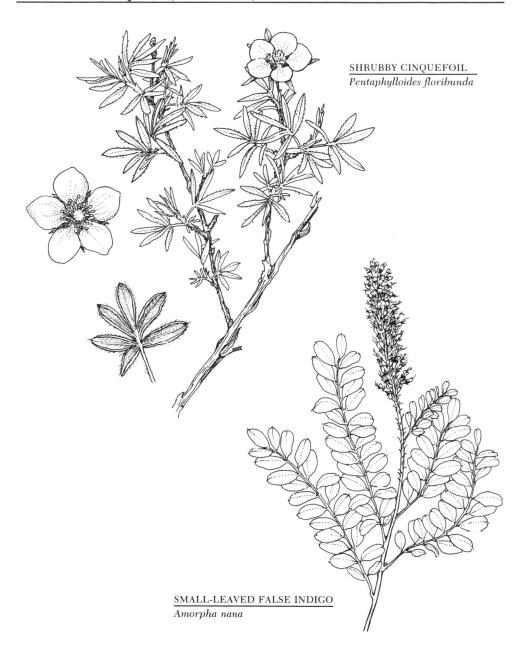

SHRUBBY CINQUEFOIL
Pentaphylloides floribunda

SMALL-LEAVED FALSE INDIGO
Amorpha nana

7.   Leaves nearly all sessile; leaflets 15 to 31 per leaf, 0.5 to 1.7 cm long; fruit 1-seeded; low shrubs rarely over 1.0 m tall; rare in Colorado on the mesas and prairie from 5,000 to 7,200 ft (1524 to 2195 m).

SMALL-LEAVED FALSE INDIGO, *Amorpha nana* Nutt.   (Fabaceae)

7.   Leaves petiolate; leaflets 7 to 25 per leaf, 1.8 to 4.0 cm long; fruit with 1 to many seeds; tall shrubs usually over 1.5 m tall 8

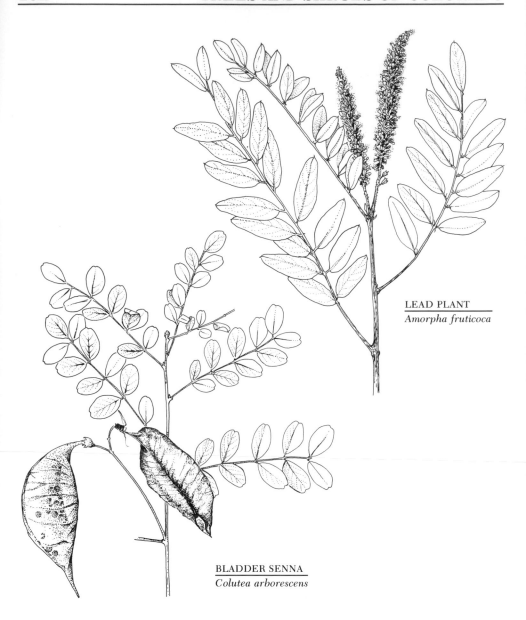

LEAD PLANT
Amorpha fruticoca

BLADDER SENNA
Colutea arborescens

8. Leaflets 7 to 13 per leaf; flowers yellow; fruit an air-filled bladder pod, 5.0 to 6.5 cm long, seeds many; cultivated and escaping cultivation in Colorado Springs.

BLADDER SENNA, *Colutea arborescens* L.   (Fabaceae)

8. Leaflets 9 to 25 per leaf; flowers dark blue or purple; fruit pods, 0.7 to 0.8 cm long, flattened, usually 2 seeds; native to the plains from 4,000 to 6,000 ft (1219 to 1829 m).

LEAD PLANT, *Amorpha fruticosa* L.   (Fabaceae)

HOP TREE
Ptelea trifoliata

9.   Leaves 7.0 to 12.0 cm long; leaflets ovate, elliptic or widest near the outer end; twigs pubescent when young becoming smooth with raised lenticels; fruit a straw-colored circular samara; south of Colorado Springs from 5,000 to 9,000 ft (1524 to 2743 m).

HOP TREE, *Ptelea trifoliata* L.   (Rutaceae)

9.   Leaves less than 4.0 cm long; leaflets linear to oblong; twigs silky-villous when young, becoming brown and shredding or peeling with age; fruit an achene; montane to subalpine, 7,000 to 11,500 ft (2134 to 3505 m).

SHRUBBY CINQUEFOIL, *Pentaphylloides floribunda* (Pursh) A. Love   (Rosaceae)

10.   Plants with spines or thorns on leaves or stems 11

10.   Plants without spines or thorns on leaves or stems 19

11.   Spines on the leaflet tips and margins 12

11.   Spines on the stems 13

12.   Shrubs trailing, growing close to the ground, less than 0.5 m tall; leaflets 3 to 7 per leaf, bluish-green above, glaucous below; native evergreen of our region; common on dry slopes, foothills to upper montane, 6,000 to 10,000 ft (1829 to 3048 m).

OREGON GRAPE, *Mahonia repens* (Lindl.) G. Don   (Berberidaceae)

OREGON GRAPE
Mahonia repens

12.   Shrubs erect, 0.5 to 2.0 m tall; leaflets 5 to 9 per leaf, shiny; cultivated evergreen in lawns and gardens of our region.

OREGON GRAPE, *Mahonia aquifolium* (Pursh) Nutt.   (Berberidaceae)

WILD RED RASPBERRY
Rubus idaeus

13. Leaves usually trifoliate occasionally with 5 leaflets; leaflet white-tomentose below, apices acute to acuminate; flowers white, 1.0 cm or less in diameter; fruit an aggregate; moist ravines; foothills to subalpine. *Rubus occidentalis* L. may also key to this species.

WILD RED RASPBERRY, *Rubus idaeus* L.   (Rosaceae)

13. Leaves usually with 5 or more leaflets; leaflet not white-tomentose below, apices obtuse to acute; flowers red, pink, occasionally yellow, rarely white, more than 1.0 cm in diameter; fruit an achene, several per flower, enclosed within a fleshy hypanthium (genus *Rosa* L.) 14

14. Flowers single; petals 5, red or pink, rarely white; shrubs native to Colorado (wild roses) 15

14. Flowers double; petals 10 or more, ranging from scarlet or violet to pink, yellow, or white; shrubs cultivated, common in lawns or gardens (horticultural hybrid varieties of roses).

HORTICULTURAL OR HYBRID ROSES, *Rosa* L. spp.   (Rosaceae)

15.　Infrastipular prickles present (these are 1 to 2 prickles situated on the twig just below the node) 16

15.　Infrastipular prickles absent 17

16.　Stems less bristly or with scattered weak prickles, often dying back in winter; leaflet margin doubly serrate with glandular teeth; flowers solitary, rarely 2 to 4 in corymbs; pedicels 19.0 to 23.0 mm long; petals 1.9 to 3.5 cm long, pink or white; occurring on plains and foothills, 3,500 to 10,000 ft (1067 to 3048 m).

NOOTKA ROSE, *Rosa nutkana* Presl.　　　　　　　(Rosaceae)

16.　Stems with numerous bristles, not dying back in winter; leaflet margin serrate to entire near base; flowers 3 or more in corymbs, less often solitary; pedicels 10.0 to 19.0 mm long; petals 1.0 to 2.5 cm long, pink; occurring in sandy soils in rocky ravines, streambanks, open prairies, or near margins of woods, 3,500 to 10,000 ft (1067 to 3048 m).

WOOD'S ROSE, WILD ROSE, *Rosa woodsii* Lindl.　　　　(Rosaceae)

WOOD'S ROSE, WILD ROSE
Rosa woodsii

17.   Stems lacking prickles, with bristles at least near base; leaflets 1.0 to 3.0 cm long, margins with glandular teeth; petals with notched apices; occurring on sandy or clay soils, in rocky ravines, streambanks, open prairies, or near margins of woods, 3,500 to 10,000 ft (1067 to 3048 m).

WOOD'S ROSE, WILD ROSE, *Rosa woodsii* Lindl.   (Rosaceae)

17.   Stems with bristles and/or prickles to apex; leaflets 1.0 to 5.0 cm long, margins without glandular teeth; petals lacking notched apices 18

18.   Shrubs less than 50.0 cm in height; stems often dying back in winter; leaflets 9 to 11 per leaf; flowers few to several in corymbs, on basal shoots or on lateral shoots from old wood; petals 1.5 to 2.5 cm long; calyx lobes lanceolate; fruit (hip) subglobose, not tapering to apex; occurring on rocky slopes and dry prairies, often in thickets, 3,500 to 9,000 ft (1067 to 2743 m).

ARKANSAS ROSE, *Rosa arkansana* Porter   (Rosaceae)

18.   Shrubs over 50.0 cm in height; stems not dying back in winter; leaflets 5 to 9 per leaf; flowers 1 to 3, always on lateral shoots from old wood; petals 2.5 to 3.0 cm long; calyx lobes 3.0 mm wide at base, narrowed near middle, and usually expanded at tip; fruit (hip) pear-shaped, tapering to apex; occurring on wooded hillsides, streambanks, and rock ledges, 4,500 to 10,000 ft (1372 to 3048 m).

PRICKLY ROSE, WILD ROSE, *Rosa acicularis* Lindl.   (Rosaceae)

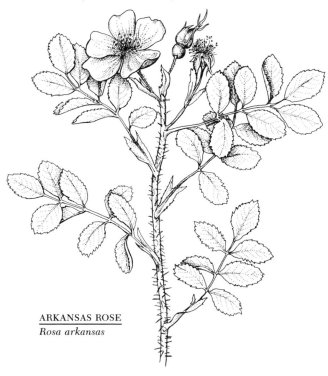

ARKANSAS ROSE
Rosa arkansas

19.   Leaves palmately compound; leaflets 3 to 5, sometimes 7 per leaf 20

19.   Leaves pinnately compound; leaflets 7 or more per leaf 24

    20.   Leaflets 5 to 7; plants woody vines 21

    20.   Leaflets 3, trifoliate; plants shrubs. (You may be working with poison
        ivy. Handle with care.) 22

21.   Tendrils ending in adhesive somewhat circular disks, branching several
times with flattened tips; leaves dull green above; cultivated and commonly
climbing on buildings.

VIRGINIA CREEPER, *Parthenocissus quinquefolia* (L.) Planch.   (Vitaceae)

21.   Tendrils with few if any adhesive disks, branching once or twice, without
flattened tips; leaves shiny green above; native to the canyons on the
mesas and foothills in southern Colorado, from 4,500 to 7,500 ft (1372 to
2286 m).

VIRGINIA CREEPER, *Parthenocissus inserta* (Kerner) K. Fritsch   (Vitaceae)

    22.   Fruit at maturity a dry, straw-colored circular samara; 1.0 to 2.0 cm
        long; inflorescence a compound cyme often becoming corymbose;
        leaves 9.0 to 15.0 cm long; leaflets ovate, elliptic or widest near the
        outer end; twigs pubescent when young becoming smooth with
        raised lenticels; in canyons on woods slopes 5,000 to 9,000 ft (1524
        to 2743 m) south of Colorado Springs. (See illustration, page 133.)

    HOP TREE, *Ptelea trifoliata* L.   (Rutaceae)

    22.   Fruit at maturity a dry, one-seeded globular, white, cream colored,
        red or orange drupe; inflorescence a panicle 23

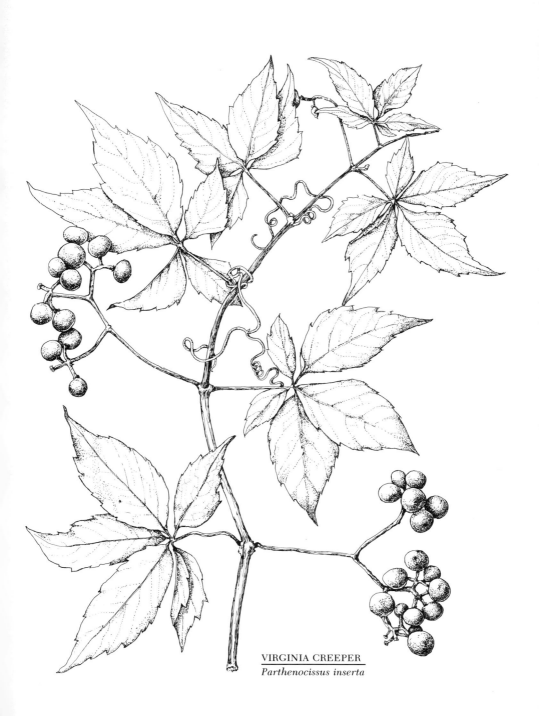

VIRGINIA CREEPER
Parthenocissus inserta

23. Leaflets 1.0 to 3.0 cm long, margins shallow crenate to rounded lobes; terminal leaflet sessile; fruit red to orange, pubescent, in dense panicles; plant an erect shrub; native to mesas and foothills from 4,000 to 9,000 ft (1219 to 2713 m).

SKUNKBRUSH, *Rhus aromatica* Ait. ssp. *trilobata* Nutt.　　(Anacardiaceae)

SKUNKBRUSH
Rhus aromatica

23. Leaflets 3.0 to 20.0 cm long, margins serrate; terminal leaflet petiolate; fruit white to cream colored, glabrous, in loose panicles; plant ranging from an erect shrub to a woody vine; native to open hillsides, roadsides and thickets from 4,000 to 9,000 ft (1219 to 2743 m). A high percentage of people are allergic to this plant.

POISON IVY, POISON OAK, *Toxicodendron rydbergii* (Small ex Rydb.) Greene   (Anacardiaceae)

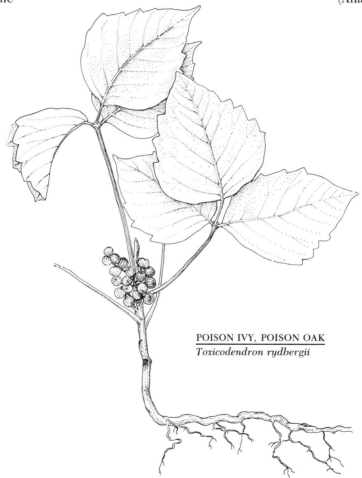

POISON IVY, POISON OAK
Toxicodendron rydbergii

24. Leaflets ovate, often lobed; petiolule on larger mature leaflets up to 3.0 mm in length; flowers yellow; fruit a papery capsule, up to 5.0 cm long; seeds black; small cultivated tree.

GOLDENRAIN TREE, *Koelreuteria paniculata* Laxm.   (Sapindaceae)

24. Leaflets usually lanceolate, never lobed, commonly sessile; petiolule, if present, less than 3.0 mm long; flowers green, yellow-green, or white; fruit variable, usually nuts, nutlets, or berries, never a papery capsule 25

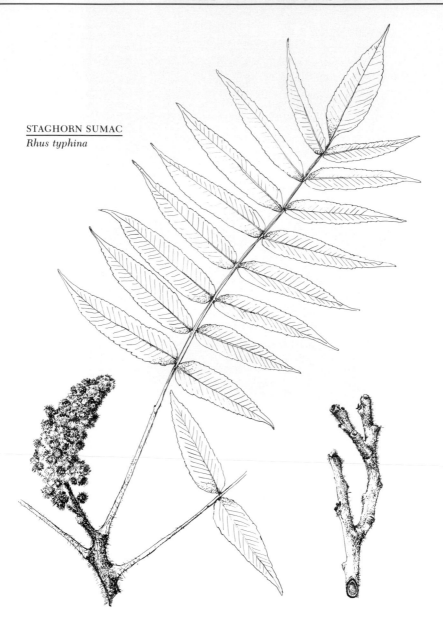

STAGHORN SUMAC
Rhus typhina

25.   Mature stems and rachises densely pilose; leaves 25.0 to 60.0 cm long; leaflets 11 to 31 per leaf lanceolate; fruit a drupe, densely pilose, arranged in panicles; pith solid, never chambered; a small introduced, cultivated tree in our area.

      STAGHORN SUMAC, *Rhus typhina* L.   (Anacardiaceae)

25.   Mature stems and rachises not densely pilose or obviously hairy, if pubescent then pubescence only found on younger twigs and in the inflorescence; leaflets 9 to 21 per leaf; fruit a nut, drupe, or berry. 26

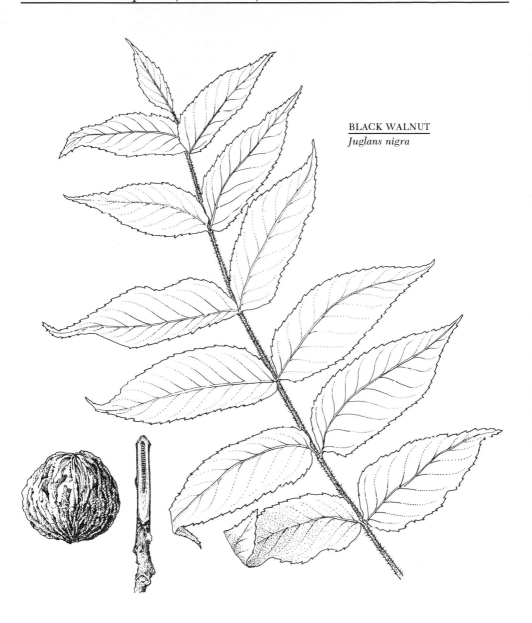

BLACK WALNUT
Juglans nigra

26.   Trees tall, at maturity up to 23.0 m in our area; pith in twigs chambered; plants monoecious; flowers imperfect; inflorescence a staminate catkin or small clusters of 2 to 4 pistillate flowers; fruit a nut enclosed in an indehiscent husk; cultivated in our area.

   BLACK WALNUT, *Juglans nigra* L.   (Juglandaceae)

26.   Trees or shrubs, at maturity not over 8.0 m in our area; pith in twigs continuous; flowers perfect or imperfect; inflorescence a panicle or corymb; fruit a drupe or a berry, never a nut 26

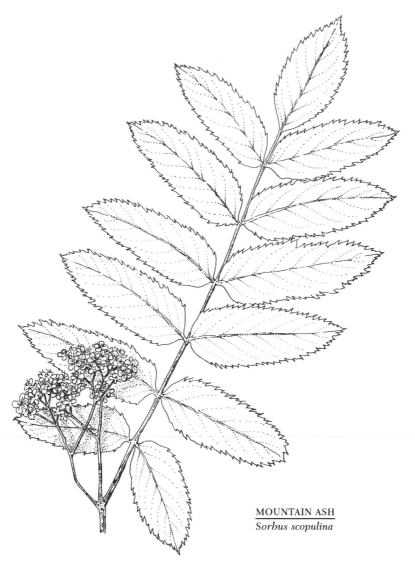

MOUNTAIN ASH
Sorbus scopulina

27.   Leaflets 9 to 13 per leaf, oblong to ovate, finely toothed; flowers perfect;
      inflorescence a corymb; fruit a berry, orange; native to rocky canyons and
      ravines from 6,000 to 10,000 ft (1829 to 3048 m), but also cultivated in
      our area. Cultivated species may be *Sorbus aucuparia* L.

MOUNTAIN ASH, *Sorbus scopulina* Greene   (Rosaceae)

27.   Leaflets 15 to 23 per leaf, lanceolate to slightly ovate, broadly toothed;
      flowers imperfect; inflorescence in pyramidal panicle terminating leafy
      twigs; fruit a drupe, red to dark brown; found on slopes, in valleys, and
      in the foothills, 5,000 to 7,500 ft (1524 to 2286 m); sometimes cultivated
      in our area.

SMOOTH SUMAC, *Rhus glabra* L.   (Anacardiaceae)

Glossary

abortive - rudimentary, arrested in development, unsuccessful, fruitless

achene - a one-seeded, dry, indehiscent fruit with seed attached to fruit wall at one point only (see Plate V)

accrescent - growing after flowering or bud development has occurred, enlarged with age

acuminate - tapering to a long point with straight or convex margins terminal angle less than 45′ (see Plate III)

acute - pointed with straight or convex margins, terminal angle 45′ to 90′ (see Plate III)

aggregate (fruit) - a group of separate fruits formed from one flower

alkaline - containing or having the properties of soluble mineral salts found in soils; having a basic pH i.e., greater than 7 (opposite of acidic)

alternate - one leaf or other structure per node (see Plate I)

anthesis - point in time when the flower expands and opens

appressed - lying-flat

aristate - having an awn; with a straight stiff extension more than 3:1 length:width ratio

attenuate - tapering to a long point with concave margins, terminal angle less than 45′ (see Plate III)

awl-shaped - narrow and tapering to a sharp point (see Plate II)

axil (or axile) - the upper angle formed between two structures, i.e., upper angle where a leaf joins the stem (see Plate I)

axilliary - in the axil; leaves, flowers, or other structures borne in the axil

axis - the main stem of a plant or inflorescence

barbed - with short, rigid, reflexed bristles

basal sheath - closely imbricated bud scales at the base of a fascicle or cluster of needles

beak (fruit) - the persistent style base on fruit

berry - a fleshy fruit with a succulent fruit wall, such as a tomato (see Plate V)

bi- - a prefix meaning two or twice, e.g. "bipinnate" twice pinnate

blade - the expanded portion of a leaf (see Plate I)

bloom - whitish powdery covering on a surface, easily rubbed off

bract - modified reduced leaf subtending a flower, flower cluster, or cone scales

bristly - covered with stiff, strong hairs

bud - an immature vegetative or floral shoot usually enclosed by scales (see Plate I)

bud scars - a mark indicating former attachment of a bud (see Plate I)

bundle scars - a mark indicating former place of attachment within the leaf scar of the vascular bundle or vein (see Plate I)

callous - having a thickened, raised area which is usually hard

calyx - the lowermost outer collective whorl on a flower, sepals (see Plate V)

campanulate - shaped like a bell

canescent - covered with dense, fine, grayish-white hairs

capsule - dry dehiscent fruit derived from two or more carpels (see Plate V)

carpel - a component or highly modified leaf comprising the female reproductive part of the flower *catkin* - a specialized scaly spike type inflorescence, often pendulous of apetalous and unisexual flowers as in the birches and willows

caudate - forming a tail or tail-like tip or appendage

caudex - a short, thickened, often woody, base of a perennial plant, usually subterranean or at ground level

ciliate - with hairs protruding from the margins

clasping - partly surrounding the stem or other structure

cleft - indentations or incisions cut 1/4 to 1/2 the distance to the midrib or midvien

compound - composed of 2 or more parts; in leaves, with leaf divided into two or more segments (see Plate IV)

cone - in gymnosperms, the fruit consisting of a stiff axis and leaf-like scales bearing ovules or pollen

conical - shaped like a true cone

cordate - heart-shaped, referring to the shape of a leaf or leaf base

corolla - whorl of petals, located above the calyx (see Plate V)

corymb - a flat-topped or convex indeterminate cluster of flowers in which the pedicels, or flower stalks, are of unequal length with the lower stalks longer (see Plate VI)

crenate - shallowly, ascending, round-toothed margin, teeth cut less than 1/8 the distance to midrib or midvein (see Plate III)

crenulate - diminutive of crenate, teeth cut less than 1/16 the distance to midrib or midvein

cuneate - widely acuminate, margins straight or convex forming a terminal angle less than 45' (see Plate III)

cylindric - long, tubular shape

cyme - a flat-topped or rounded, determinate inflorescence of stalked flowers in which the central flower is the oldest (see Plate VI)

deciduous - persistent for one growing season; falling off, as leaves that are shed in autumn

dehiscent(fruit) - one that splits open (see Plate V)

deltoid - broadly triangular, length:depth ratio 1:1 (see Plate II)

dentate - margins with rounded or sharp coarse teeth that point outwards at right angles to midrib or midvein, teeth cut to 1/8 the distance to midrib or midvein (see Plate III)

denticulate - diminutive of dentate, teeth cut to 1/16 the distance to midrib or midvein

depressed - pressed down, flattened vertically

diffuse - spread over wide surface; with many loose or open branches

dioecious - plants with imperfect flowers, but staminate and pistillate flowers on separate plants

disk - in flowers, an enlargement of the floral axis developed near base of the pistil or the ovary; in tendrils, a flattened portion of tendril, usually adhesive (see Plate VI)

dissected - irregularly cut into numerous segments

disturbed (habitat) - habitats that have been interfered with, interrupted, or broken up, as in cultivated fields, railroads, roadsides, dry waste places, or rubbish heaps

downy - covered with short, weak, soft hairs

drupe - a fleshy fruit with a stony inner fruit wall, as in cherries (see Plate V)

drupelets - a small drupe, as in gooseberries or currants

elliptic - a longer than wide shape with the widest axis at the midpoint of the structure and with margins symmetrically curved (see Plate II)

entire - without indentations or incisions on margins; smooth (see Plate III)

epidermis - the outermost layer of cells of a leaf, stem, or other structure

evergreen - bearing green leaves throughout the winter, leaves persistent two or more growing seasons

exerted - projecting beyond surrounding structures or parts

fascicles - cluster or bundle often with commonly attached parts (see Plate IV)

filiform - thread-like (see Plate II)

fleshy - in fruits, having a firm pulp; pulpy

follicles - a dry dehiscent fruit derived from one carpel that splits open along one suture or seam (see Plate V)

fruit - a ripened mature ovary, sometimes including other floral parts

glabrous - smooth, lacking hairs or pubescence

gland - a secretory hair or other part that produces a liquid, such as nectar

glandular - covered with minute blackish to translucent glands

glaucous - covered with a bloom, or smooth waxy coating

globose - round, spherical in form

globular - nearly globose

glossy - having a smooth, shiny, polished surface

granular - composed of granules

granule - a small grain-like particle or spot

habitat - native environment; region where a plant or animal naturally occurs

head - a dense inflorescence of sessile or subsessile flowers on a short or broadened compound receptacle (see Plate VI)

heartwood - the non-living and commonly dark-colored wood in which no water transport occurs; found at the core of the wood and surrounded by sapwood

hemispheric - shaped like half of a sphere or globe

herbaceous - like an herb, not woody; soft and succulent

hispid - covered with long stiff bristles or hairs

hull - the outer covering of a seed or fruit, as in the pod of peas

husk - the dry outer covering of various fruits or seeds, as in an ear of corn

hypanthium - fused or coalesced basal portion of floral parts (sepals, petals, stamens) around the ovary (see Plate V)

imbedded - to set in a surrounding mass or part

imbricate - with overlapping edges or margins

imperfect - flowers with either stamens or pistils absent; unisexual flowers

incised - margins sharply or deeply cut, usually jaggedly (see Plate III)

indehiscent - not splitting open (see Plate V)

inedible - not edible; unfit to eat

inferior - floral arrangement in which the ovary is situated below the point of insertion of the other flower parts (see Plate V)

inflorescence - an arrangement or cluster of flowers

infrastipular - on the stem below the leaves

internodes - portion of the stem between two adjacent nodes, usually lacking leaves and buds (see Plate I)

involucre - a group or cluster of bracts subtending in inflorescence or flower cluster *keeled* - sharply creased or ridged

lanceolate - shaped like the head of a lance; elongate with widest axis below middle and with margins symmetrically curved (see Plate II)

lateral - on the side of a structure

leaf scar - mark indicating former attachment of a leaf (see Plate I)

leaflet - one of the divisions of a compound leaf (see Plate I)

legume - a usually dry dehiscent fruit derived from one carpel that splits along two sutures (see Plate V)

lenticel - a pore in the bark (see Plate I)

ligule - the united corolla of a ray flower, common in the Asteraceae family

linear - long and narrow with parallel margins, length:width ratio greater than 10:1 (see Plate II)

lobe - a partial division of a leaf or other structure; any, usually rounded, segment or part of the perianth

lobed - large round-toothed, cut 1/8 to 1/4 the distance to midvein (see Plate III)

locule - cavity or compartment within an ovary or anther (see Plate V)

lustrous - glossy, shiny

mealy - powdery, dry, soft

midrib, midvein - main or central vein of a leaf or other structure (see Plate I)

monoecious - plant with all flowers imperfect, but staminate and pistillate flowers on same plant

multiple fruit - fruit derived from several flowers, as in mulberries or figs

naked - lacking organs or parts, e.g. a naked bud lacks scales

netted(veins) - with veins forming a network

nodding - bending or swaying back and forth, or up and down

node - region on stem where a leaf, leaves, or branches arise (see Plate I)

nut - a one-seeded, dry, indehiscent fruit with a hard fruit wall, as in acorns or walnuts (see Plate V)

nutlet - a small nut

oblanceolate - inversely lanceolate; elongate with widest axis above middle (see Plate II)

oblique - having an asymmetrical base (see Plate III)

oblong - elongate with more or less parallel margins, length:width ratio usually less than 10:1 (see Plate II)

obovate - inversely ovate; egg-shaped with the widest axis above the middle (see Plate II)

obtuse - blunt with margins straight or convex, forming a terminal angle more than 90' (see Plate III)

opposite - two leaves or other structures per node, on opposite sides of stem or central axis (see Plate I)

orbicular - flat with a circular appearance (see Plate II)

oval - broadly elliptic (see Plate II)

ovary - ovule-bearing part of pistil, usually near base of pistil (see Plate V)

ovate - egg-shaped; with widest axis below middle and margins symmetrically curved (see Plate II)

ovoid - a 3-dimensional egg-shaped figure with the widest exis below the middle and the margins symmetrically curved

ovule - embryonic seed, structure that develops into the seed after fertilization (see Plate V) *palmate* - radiately lobed, divided or shaped; with parts diverging from a common base (see Plate IV)

panicle - a branched inflorescence with pedicelled flowers (see Plate VI)

parallel - extending in the same direction and at the same distance apart at every point

parted - indentations or incisions cut 1/2 to 3/4 the distance to the midrib (see Plate III)

pedicel - individual flower stalk

pedicellate - with a pedicel or flower stalk

peduncle - main stalk for the entire inflorescence

peltate - having the stalk or petiole attached underneath near the center of the underside of structure or leaf blade (see Plate II)

pendulous - hanging loosely or freely downward

perfect - with both stamens and pistils present in flower

perianth - refers to the calyx and the corolla collectively; combined sepals and petals (see Plate V)

persistent - remaining attached, not falling or shedding

petals - a corolla member or segment; a unit of the corolla (see Plate V)

petiolate - with a petiole or leaf stalk

petiole - leaf stalk (see Plate I)

petiolule - leaflet stalk (see Plate I)

phyllary - an involucral bract in the Asteraceae family, several phyllaries surrounding a head of flowers (see Plate VI)

pilose - with long soft shaggy hairs

pinnate - arranged on both sides of a common axis; arranged like a feather (see Plate IV)

pinnatifid - cut pinnately

pistil - the female reproductive part of a flower, composed of one to several carpels (see Plate V)

pistillate - with pistils or carpels only in the flower, lacking stamens

pith - centermost tissue or region of a stem (see Plate I)

plumose - feather-like

pod - the hull or seed case of peas, beans, and other legumes

polygamo-dioecious - plants dioecious, but with some perfect flowers on staminate or pistillate plants or both

pome - a berry-like fruit fused to a fleshy receptacle and with a bony or leathery inner fruit wall, as in apples (see Plate V)

prickles - a sharp-pointed outgrowth from the epidermis or cortex of a structure

procumbent - trailing or lying flat, not rooting at the nodes

prostrate - trailing or lying flat, not rooting at the nodes

pruinose - frosted, with a heavy wax coat

puberulent - minutely pubescent

pubescent - covered with dense or scattered hairs, hairs usually straight and slender hairs

punctate - covered with minute impressions or depressions

pyramidal - a 3-dimensional short triangular figure, with length:depth ratio 2:3 to 1:3 or more

raceme - unbranched indeterminate inflorescence with stalked flowers (see Plate VI)

rachis - major axis within an inflorescence

ray flowers - strap-shaped or ligulate flowers, common in head inflorescences (see Plate VI) *receptacle* - the extended portion of the floral axis which bears and supports the flower parts (see Plate V)

reflexed - directed backwards, bent or turned downwards

resin duct - a tube-like intercellular space secreting or containing resin

resin - a solid or semisolid substance exuded from plants

resinous - having a yellowish, sticky exudate or discharge

reticulate - netted

revolute - margins or outer portion of sides rolled outward or downwards over lower or dorsal surface; margins rolled under (see Plate III)

rhizome - a horizontal underground stem

rhombic - with widest axis at midpoint of structure and with straight margins; diamond-shaped (see Plate II)

rosette - a circular cluster of leaves, petals or other structures

rotate - wheel-shaped, with a short tube and wide lobe at right angles to tube

rotund - rounded or rounded-out; plump

rudimentary - incompletely or imperfectly developed; vestigial

saccate - pouch-like

saline - salty; containing or characteristic of salt

samara - a winged dry fruit (see Plate V)

scabrous - having a harsh surface, rough to touch

scale - small protective non-green leaf on outside of bud; overlapping thin, flat, flaky or plate-like structures

scaly - covered with or composed of scales

scape - naked peduncle; a naked flowering stem with or without a few scale leaves

scurfy - with scaly incrustations, covered with small bran-like scales

seed - a mature ovule

sepals - a calyx member or segment; a unit of the calyx (see Plate V)

septicidal capsule - a capsule that dehisces longitudinally through the septa or dividing wall

serrate - saw-toothed; teeth sharp and ascending, cut 1/16 to 1/8 the distance to midrib or midvein (see Plate III)

serrulate - dimunitive of serrate, teeth cut to 1/16 the distance to midrib or midvein

sessile - without a petiole, petiolule, or stalk

shiny - lustrous, polished, glossy

simple - undivided, not composed of more than one structurally equivalent unit

sinus - space or recess between two lobes or partition of a leaf

smooth - without any configuration; lacking projections or roughness

solitary - simple, without others; one flower, not an inflorescence (see Plate VI)

spatulate - oblong or obovate apically with an attenuate base (see Plate II)

spikes - unbranched, indeterminate elongate, inflorescence with sessile flowers (see Plate VI)

spine - sharp-pointed petiole, midrib, vein, or stipule; a sharp, slender, rigid outgrowth

spur - a short shoot on which flowers, fruits or leaves are borne; a tubular or pointed projection from the perianth

stamen - the floral organ that bears the pollen in flowering plants; the male reproductive part of a flower (see Plate V)

staminate - with stamens only in the flower, lacking pistils *stellate* - star-shaped

stigma - the tip of the pistil that receives the pollen, attached directly to the style (see Plate V)

stipules - paired scales, spines, glands, or blade-like structures at the base of a petiole (see Plate I)

striate - with longitudinal lines

style - attenuated portion of pistil betweeen the ovary and the stigma (see Plate V)

sub- - prefix meaning almost slightly, e.g. "subcordate" slightly cordate; prefix meaning under, below, e.g. "subterranean" below ground

succulent - having juicy tissues, as in cactus

superior - flower arrangement in which the other floral organs are attached below ovary (see Plate V)

symmetrical - having a similarity in form or arrangement

talus - a slope composed of rocks and rock fragments

tendril - a long slender coiling branch, adapted for climbing (see Plate IV)

terminal - at the tip or end of a branch or other structure

ternate - occurring in sets of three ternately (see Plate IV)

thorn - a sharp-pointed branch

tomentose - covered with dense interwoven hairs

trailing - sprawling on ground, usually with adventious roots

translucent - shiny, partially transparent as in frosted glass; allows light to pass through but diffuses it so that objects can not be distinguished clearly

trifoliate - a compound leaf with 3 leaflets (see Plate IV)

triternate - with three orders of leaflets, each ternately compound (see Plate IV)

truncate - cut straight across; ending abruptly almost at right angles to midrib or midvein

tube - the cylindrical part of an united corolla or calyx

tubular - cylindrical

twining - twisted around a central object; coiling around an object

umbel - a determinate or indeterminate, flat-topped or convex inflorescence with the pedicels arising from a common point (see Plate VI)

umbellate - resembling an umbel

undulate - wavy in a vertical plane, with a series of vertical curves at right angles to the central axis (see Plate III)

unisexual - with only one sex in each flower; with stamens or carpels absent in the flower

utricle - a small, bladdery or inflated, one-seeded, dry fruit

valvate - having margins of adjacent structures touching at edges only, not overlapping

vein - any vascular bundle forming the framework of a leaf blade

veinlet - a small vein

ventral - inner face of an organ; upper surface of a leaf; adaxial

villous - covered with long, soft, crooked hairs

vine - an elongate, weak-stemmed, often climbing plant

warty - with lumps, like warts

whorl - a cyclic or acyclic group of leaves, petals, sepals, or other structures; a group of three or more leaves, or other structures, per node (see Plate I)

wing - a flattened extension, projection, or appendage

woody - hard and lignified

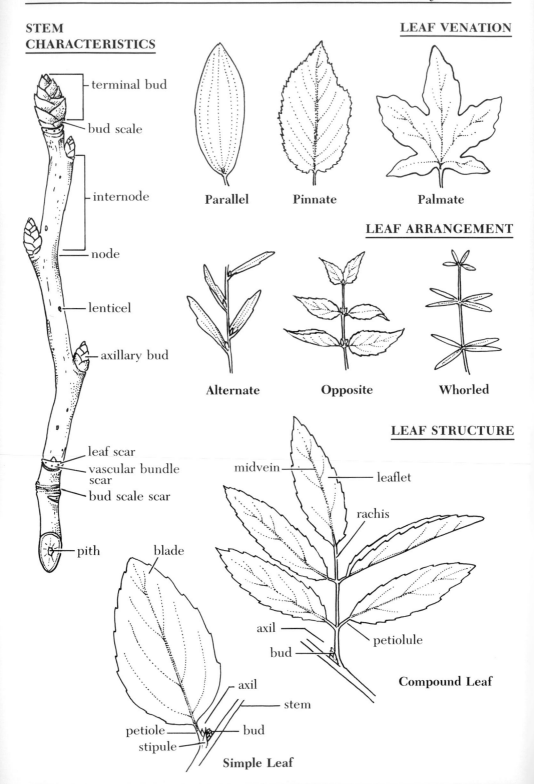

STEM CHARACTERISTICS

- terminal bud
- bud scale
- internode
- node
- lenticel
- axillary bud
- leaf scar
- vascular bundle scar
- bud scale scar
- pith

LEAF VENATION

Parallel   Pinnate   Palmate

LEAF ARRANGEMENT

Alternate   Opposite   Whorled

LEAF STRUCTURE

- midvein
- leaflet
- rachis
- axil
- bud
- petiolule

Compound Leaf

- blade
- axil
- stem
- petiole
- bud
- stipule

Simple Leaf

LEAF SHAPES

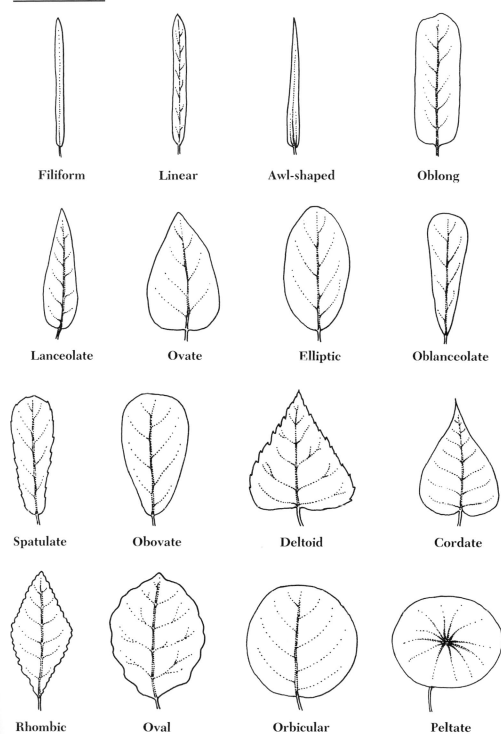

Filiform   Linear   Awl-shaped   Oblong

Lanceolate   Ovate   Elliptic   Oblanceolate

Spatulate   Obovate   Deltoid   Cordate

Rhombic   Oval   Orbicular   Peltate

LEAF APICES

Acuminate   Caudate   Acute   Obtuse   Cordate

LEAF BASES

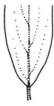
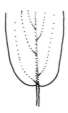

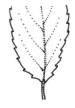

Attenuate   Cuneate   Obtuse   Rounded   Oblique

LEAF MARGINS

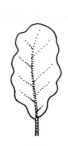
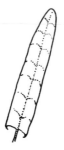
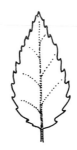

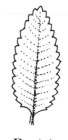

Entire   Undulate   Revolute   Serrate   Biserrate   Dentate

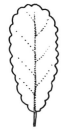
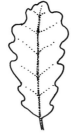
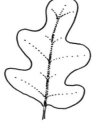
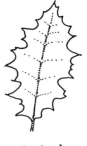

Crenate   Lobed   Divided   Incised

LEAF MODIFICATION

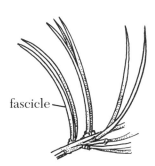

Tendril   **Scale-like**   **Needle-like**

COMPOUND LEAVES

Even Pinnate

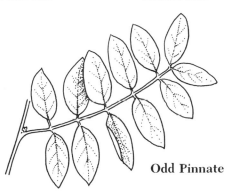

Odd Pinnate

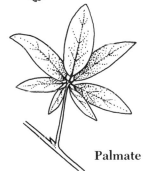

Palmate

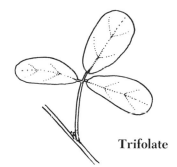

Trifolate

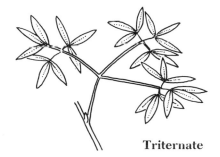

Triternate

FLOWER STRUCTURE

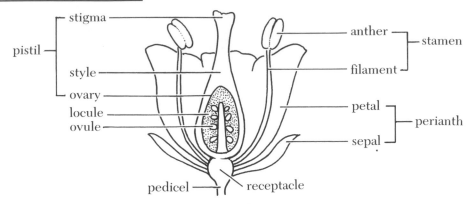

OVARY POSITION

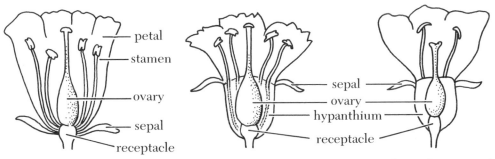

Superior (hypogenous)   **Superior (perigenous)**   **Inferior (epigynous)**

FRUIT TYPES

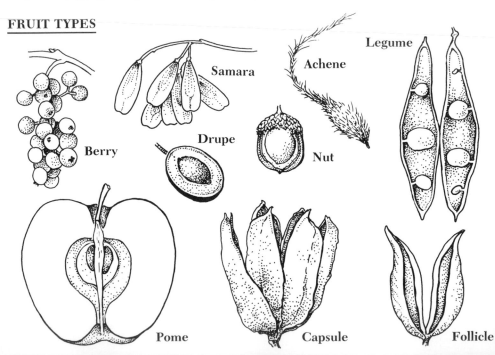

Berry Samara Drupe Achene Nut Legume Pome Capsule Follicle

INFLORESCENCES

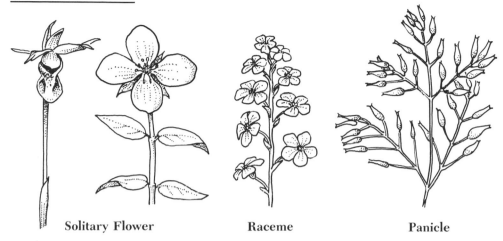

Solitary Flower   **Raceme**   **Panicle**

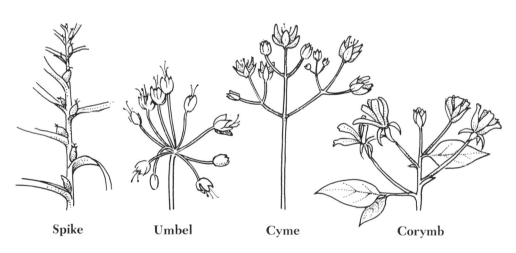

Spike   **Umbel**   **Cyme**   **Corymb**

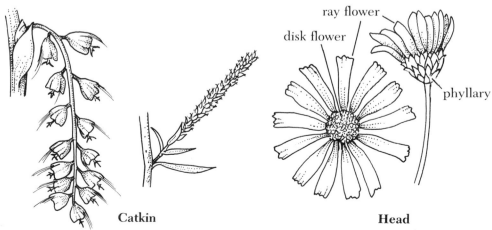

ray flower

disk flower

phyllary

Catkin   **Head**

References

Dorn, Robert D. 1977. *Manual of the Vascular Plants of Wyoming. Vol. I-II*. Garland Publishing, Inc.

Gleason, H.A. 1952. *The New Britton and Brown Illustrated Flora of Northeastern United States and Adjacent Canada. Vol. I-III*. New York Botanical Garden.

Harrington, H.D. 1954. *Manual of the Plants of Colorado*. Sage Books.

Kelly, George W. 1970. *A Guide to the Woody Plants of Colorado*. Pruett Publishing Company.

Kelly, George W. 1979. *Shrubs for the Rocky Mountains*. Rocky Mountain Horticultural Publishing Company, Inc.

Kingsbury, John M. 1964. *Poisonous Plants of the United States and Canada*. 626 pages. Prentice Hall, Inc.

Lamb, Samuel H. 1971. *Woody Plants of New Mexico*. New Mexico Department of Game and Fish.

Marr, John W. 1961. *Ecosystems of the East Slope of the Front Range in Colorado*. University of Colorado Studies, Series in Biology, No. 8:1-134.

Martin, W.C. & C.R. Hutchins. 1980. *A Flora of New Mexico. Vol. I-II*. A.R. Gantner Verlag K.G. (J. Cramer).

McGregor, Ronald L. (Coordinator) & T.M. Barkley (Editor). 1986. *Flora of the Great Plains*. University of Kansas Press.

Mutel, Cornelia F. & John C. Emerick. 1984. *From Grassland to Glacier*. Johnson Publishing Company.

Nelson, Ruth Ashton. 1961. *Plants of Rocky Mountain National Park*. U.S. Government Printing Office, Washington.

Nelson, Ruth Ashton. 1979. *Handbook of Rocky Mountain Plants*. Skyland Publishers.

Ramaley, Francis. 1927. *Colorado Plant Life*. University of Colorado Press.

Rydberg, P.A. 1906. *Flora of Colorado*. Bulletin 100, Colorado Agricultural Experiment Station.

Rydberg, P.A. 1922. *Flora of the Rocky Mountains and Adjacent Plains*. Published by author.

Scoggan, H.J. 1978. *The Flora of Canada*. Parts 1-4. National Museum of Canada.

Stephens, H.A. 1973. *Woody Plants of the North Central Plains*. The University of Kansas Press.

Treshow, Michael, Stanley L. Welch and Glenn Moore. 1970. *Guide to the Woody Plants of the Mountain States*. Brigham Young University Press.

Weber, William A. 1965. *Plant Geography in the Southern Rocky Mountains*. Pp. 453-468 in The Quaternary of the United States (H.E. Wright, Jr., and David G. Frey, eds.). Princeton University Press.

Weber, William A. 1976. *Rocky Mountain Flora*. Colorado Associated University Press.

Weber, William A. 1987. *Colorado Flora, Western Slope*. Colorado Associated University Press.

Index to Common Names

Illustrations are referred to in boldface type

Index to Genera and Species

(scientific names)

Illustrations are referred to in boldface type

Index to Families

Notes